Say The Second Thing

That Comes into Your Mind

The Work and Joy of Recovery

By

JOHNNY ALLEM

Foreword By Paul Williams

ISBN 978-1-4958-2062-5
eISBN 978-1-4958-2063-2
Library of Congress Control Number: 2017915596

Published October 2017

INFINITY PUBLISHING
1094 New DeHaven Street, Suite 100
West Conshohocken, PA 19428-2713
Toll-free (877) BUY BOOK
Local Phone (610) 941-9999
Fax (610) 941-9959
Info@buybooksontheweb.com
www.buybooksontheweb.com

ACKNOWLEDGEMENTS

Countless people on recovery journeys have blessed me with their experience, strength and hopes. Their stories ring with resilience and the joy of achievement. I journal their stories of "tools" for this rewarding work. In recent years, we have seen these stories rise from private and often hidden success to celebrations that witness the fact and power of recovery.

Specific to this project, David Havsky, Peter Caulkins and Margo Warren contributed so much in editing and suggestions. I thank them for their partnership and wisdom. They are skilled communicators as well as wonderful examples of recovery.

And to Paul Williams, a partner in recovery advocacy, I am so grateful for his friendship, inspiration and unflagging example of recovery. We teamed up with U.S. Senator Harold Hughes and his efforts in the 1990s to build a public advocacy effort for addiction recovery. And we have remained partners as our field has grown to many thousands of proud and effective recovery advocates – in the United States and around the world.

Foreword By
PAUL WILLIAMS
Singer, Songwriter, Actor, Recovery Advocate

My name is Paul and I'm an alcoholic. That simple but powerful sentence, spoken for the first time twenty-seven years ago, marked the beginning of a new freedom and a new happiness for me. The wonderful life I have today was unimaginable in early sobriety.

How'd I do it? I followed a proven path to recovery created in Akron Ohio in 1935. It's a healing process and a guide for living. It continues to flourish today largely because of the willingness of those who came before to show up and share their wisdom, strength and hope with the newcomer... A choir of grateful hearts, giving away the thing they cherish most. Sobriety.

Some are exceptional in their dedication to and expertise in leading others to the good life. You're holding one hundred and ten pages of treasured truths written by one of the best.

I met Johnny Allem in the early stages of my recovery as an enthusiastic resident of the 'pink cloud' community some beginners enjoy. I loved sobriety, loved the freedom from decades of cravings, lying about the drugs, hiding from life and watching the big career I'd taken for granted beginning to shrink. Free at last I knew sober was better and I was teachable. When the student is ready the teacher will appear.

Cloaked in kindness, the strength of Johnny A. can best be described as an inherent ability to calm the storms that gather in the busy heads of addicts and alcoholics – a sometimes chaotic community he deals with on a daily basis. His leadership skills led him to boardrooms and lecterns where he has carried the message of hope for the hopeless. In Washington, DC and around the world he has devoted countless hours to educating those positioned to improve conditions for the addicted and their families. I believe he's happiest in the center of the herd, giving hands on help to the ever-growing population of alcoholics and addicts needing treatment.

Invaluable to those in recovery his 'tools' are useful in all walks of life. They are presented here with a friendly book of instructions. I especially appreciated his decision to include "Bullet Points" at the end of every chapter. Use them. They are sweet reminders that there's a better life available for all of us when lived in 'Love and Service."

I was also pleased to read his acknowledgment of Gratitude as a powerful ally in dealing with life's unavoidable difficulties. I believe that it's a miracle emotion and frankly the first word that comes to mind when I think of Johnny Allem. I'm grateful for his guidance, his friendship and for the opportunity to share my enthusiasm for his teachings with all of you. Enjoy.

Blessings and thanks,
Paul Williams

INTRODUCTION

The concept of "tools" of recovery has been crucial to my recovery journey. It implies not only that there is work to be done, but that life is not a "one and done" affair and that it is wise to keep your tools clean and handy for the next challenge.

My early life was full of farm work. My father was a preacher in several rural communities and my weekends and summers were often spent fixing fences, planting, weeding, harvesting, milking cows, and pitching hay. I was taught to respect the tools. That meant keeping track of them in the fields, washing them when finished, and placing them in their assigned storage places to be easily found for the next task.

Later, in high school, I learned to repair appliances and radios (even the early black and white television sets). My habit of respecting tools and keeping them in assigned places became very useful.

My college years were supported by working as a newspaper reporter on the night police beat. Again, I learned the importance of mental tools and strategies. I will never forget the teaching of my managing editor at the Knoxville Journal who said: "Telephones help us in our work, but have ruined many a promising reporter. Too many times we get a story on the phone, but don't really understand what we have heard. If you want to get the real story, use your feet!"

So it registered with me in my early journey in sobriety to find, use and keep handy my own tools of recovery. I benefited enormously from Twelve Step programs and philosophies. But I found other tools too, and met people who got sober through a variety of strategies and belief systems.

The concept of sponsorship was important to me. I learned it the hard way, by sponsoring myself and nearly running off the road of recovery and life. At six months without a drink or drug but still in some misery, I gave up and found someone with more experience to share my journey. Someone who shared new tools with me and taught me how to use them.

"Try every tool that is suggested," my sponsor said. "Use each tool long enough to see what happens, not just until you get tired. Keep the ones that work the best and make them part of the Johnny program. Leave the ones that don't seem so useful to you for someone else."

In this way, I learned that each of us is unique and valuable in our own way. It has been critical for me to be open to using new tools, understand why they work for me, and keep them front and center in my life.

Many of these effective tools are classics that have benefited the human race for centuries. People still find comfort and guidance from a variety of sources, including Biblical stories, Rumi sayings (a 13th Century poet popular in the US) and Chinese proverbs. But there are contemporary voices as well and I have included these.

So help yourself to my toolbox. Grab the tools that work for you. Keep them clean and handy. More importantly, be open to new teachers and tools as you navigate your recovery life. Build your own toolbox for a generous, useful and satisfying stay on this planet.

TABLE OF CONTENTS

1.

SOMETHING MISSING

I survived the first 22 years of my life without the benefit of alcohol or other mood altering chemicals. I was lonely, confused and very dissatisfied.

In my second 22 years I saw alcohol as the solution. I never quite got it right, but was always working on getting it "right." I often say I was a binge drinker: The binge started in 1960 and ended in 1982.

In 1982, I found a better solution, brought to me by connection – with other people and the spiritual universe that blesses us all. Or maybe it found me.

On my journey, I have come to realize that we are hardwired to belong to each other, to connect with each other, and to share a common spiritual calling. Most are blessed to see and exercise that asset, building social and other relationships throughout our lives. These relationships smooth the paths through growth, hardships and joys. Though often paying lip service to the "rugged individual" within us, we actually work, play and progress with mutual help and support.

Then there are people like me. My motto was "I got this."

The truth is that "I got this" damn near killed me.

I am the son of a preacher man. He brought to his particular gospel the influence of alcoholism in his family. My grandfather died of this disease. Sober during Prohibition, he returned to drink in 1933, losing his career, his home, and his relationship with nine children. Pulled from college to help restore a collapsed family, my father took the "pledge," became an evangelist, and practiced a level of sanctimony and self-righteousness that immediately and for years to come alienated his oldest child and only son.

My father also had difficulty holding a church or a job. In my early years, we lived in Keokuk, Iowa (where I was born); Albuquerque, New Mexico; Quincy, Illinois; Los Angeles, California; and Danville, Iowa – finally landing in Dayton, Tennessee, where I bonded with the mountains and the people, finding my adolescent "home."

I lived an isolated life, with few peers or friends. I learned that friendships only led to loss. A retired teacher in our church tutored me for first grade. I then found myself in Los Angeles public schools in the center city, the only white child in the entire school – except for my sister one grade behind me. I did not attend school with white children until the fifth grade and found myself, for some reason, completely uncomfortable and alienated.

I learned at an early age to deal with other children at a distance. I had learned to be a loner. To depend solely on myself, my skills and my resources. I came to believe that was not just normal, but a superior way to live. Every time I relied on someone else, I was hurt, disappointed or suffered a loss.

"I got this" seemed to work best.

As we moved from place to place, I pushed myself to develop and participate in a variety of skills and activities. At nine years old in LA, I shined shoes carrying my shine box to the front of a liquor store on Beverly Boulevard. I built scooters out of orange crates and disassembled roller skates. In Iowa, I learned to sell greeting cards door to door. In Tennessee, I played trumpet in the marching band and became a top scoring guard on my school's basketball team.

But "connection" was not part of my deal. I worked to please people. I could hold my own in a team. But, bottom line, I "did it my way," which meant I held myself accountable only to myself and shared as little as possible. Even in helping others, a service I enjoyed, relationships were more of a transaction than an expression of fellowship. I was not devoid of friendships – two or three survive even today. But in terms of benefiting from human connection, I was lost.

My journey began with surrender. And using tools to accept myself, connect with others, and find my passion. Today, I live in good health, wonderful friends, and in the grace of an understanding and teaching Higher Power. Please enjoy my experience with these tools.

Tool: **STORY**
Bullet Points:

- *Know your story.*
- *Accept change.*
- *Find how life tools work.*

2.

CONNECTION HEALS

A primary psychological symptom of addiction illness is isolation.

This symptom can precede dependence on alcohol or other drugs. On the surface, it can appear as distancing one's self from a situation, placing a shield between one's soul and the "outside" world.

The root causes of this type of isolation can range from shame and embarrassment to one's inside world view. At some point, most individuals with addiction disease feel ill-equipped to deal with life's demands, frustrated by interpersonal relations, or simply unworthy.

As the disease advances from "at-risk" stages to full dependency, isolation becomes entrenched – forming a wall, reinforcing faulty thinking, and strengthening denial. Pain associated with this separation becomes severe. The intuitive need to medicate this pain drives us to even more drinking and drugging.

While healing from addiction requires significant internal transformation, it is connection to others that restores the appropriate arrangement of human beings on the common mission of survival and wholesome living. Human beings are born to rely on each other. Few images of life are as distracting and false as the lone hero building a future through fierce independence and self-reliance.

A major reason Twelve Step groups are effective is that they provide a platform for connection. When a person suffering from addiction sees and talks with another sufferer, the healing begins.

A useful direction is initiated when one alcoholic or addict opens up to another who shares the feelings of addictive pain, but has begun the path to recovery. In time, and as trust is rewarded, the individual learns to open up to a small group in recovery. Trust is awakened as a useful tool, rather than a foolish risk.

Continuing the healing, connection expands and multiplies to restore family and work relationships. As mature recovery develops, the person on the recovery journey sees everyone differently, replacing fear with a new knowledge that we are all family, and that we share our experience, personal growth and hope with all our spiritual siblings on this unique and wonderful planet.

Tool: **CONNECTION**
Bullet Points:

- *Find root causes of isolation.*
- *Practice trust.*
- *Share the healing.*

3.

We are Valuable

Most addicted people try many times to stop drinking or drugging before they achieve success in long-term, stable recovery. There are many reasons for this. But the most significant underlying condition is simply:

We believe we are not valuable enough as human beings.

Our lives are often a treadmill of action and achievement designed to convince others that we are worthy. However, we never seem able to impress the person that really matters: our self.

As our drinking and drugging become problematic, we add guilt to the mix of why we just can't make it in this world. Often there is a malignancy inside that never allowed us to grow emotionally. The malignancy is nourished by our fears, resentments, anger and isolation and avoidance of healthy relationships. The result is stressful and unsatisfactory mastery of painful adolescent lessons and a difficult transition to mature adulthood.

As we retreat into isolation, sometimes surrounded by crowds of people, we confirm our belief that we are truly unworthy and "less than," not only in the eyes of others, but in the mirror of our self-awareness.

Reclaiming our intrinsic value is one happy result of effective treatment for addiction illness and related emotional difficulties. Reinforcing the fact of our core value is a daily task. Experience has suggested a few strategies for maintaining the correct view of our worth:

One. Associate and connect with people who value us enough to share experiences and honestly in recovery.

Two. Write down, or journal, a daily reminder of your truth and the positive reasons that demonstrate your self-worth this day. Some add a gratitude list of the day's journey

Three. Demonstrate your truth by being available to others and sharing your experience, strength and hope.

Four. Join in projects and events that celebrate holistic recovery and remind you of your value. This includes being of use to others and shouldering responsibilities to family, friends, associates and the community.

Tool: **MIRROR**
Bullet Points:

- *Stop living to impress others.*
- *Reclaim our intrinsic value.*
- *Celebrate the healing.*

4.

GET REAL
The Recovery Journey

—◄▧◯▧►—

Reality is an elusive state for many of us with addiction disease. A major reason to use chemical mood changers is to avoid what is really going on in our life. One of my favorite sayings was:

"Reality is for people who can't handle drugs or alcohol."

Avoiding reality takes several forms. Pain avoidance is one. Shame is another. Often, a mental illness makes it easier to pursue fantasies than face daily life conditions.

I can remember someone telling me in early recovery to "drop your arms." He said the effort to hold up the false image of myself was no longer necessary and my arms were probably getting tired.

At first, I could not show the real me. Since childhood, I tried to present a version of myself that would please others and convince them of my value. I took for granted that I had little intrinsic value and if people could see the real me, they would drop any interest in me or my well-being.

In recovery, the best I could do was take little steps toward reality. I remember finally trusting one person to share honestly what was going on inside me. Then a small group I learned to admire in a regular recovery meeting.

At each step, I learned two things. First, the earth did not crash when my true self emerged. Second, I am a valuable individual.

It soon emerged that even though I worked in the public relations field, I did not really enjoy other people. I was successful because I learned to "present" as others expected me to. Away from my job, I was much more comfortable isolating. People, outside my family, just didn't appeal to me.

So AA meetings were boring. I didn't relate. I might enjoy a dramatic story as entertainment, but I simply didn't connect. But I knew that I had to if I was to stop drinking.

So I got in the habit of listening to a "share" that seemed to make sense and approaching that person right after the meeting.

"Thank you for sharing," I would say. And an actual conversation would often follow. Meetings got less boring. I picked up a few numbers. And found myself actually sharing in a meeting one day.

Gradually, I dropped the image. My life became fuller. I enjoyed the adventure of meeting and sharing with others. I stopped regretting that some people just are not my type and I welcomed them to move on.

I finally reached a place where I believed "what other people think of me is none of my business." When I opened myself to reality instead of the fantasy world of my drinking mind, I could begin the work of growth, trust, acceptance and confident living.

Those who find following the Twelve Steps of AA useful to their recovery will see "getting real" as the objective of Step One: Admitting we were powerless over alcohol and that our lives had become unmanageable.

*Tool: **SEE THE UNMANAGEABLE LIFE**.*
Bullet Points:

- *Take small steps to reality.*
- *Drop your fantasy image.*
- *See your underlying value.*

5.

GET HELP
The Recovery Journey

As I mentioned earlier, my working motto was "I got this." I am one of those guys who can rent a car in a new city and drive for hours looking for an address – never thinking to ask someone for directions.

Somehow, I thought that every skill – from making a living to raising children – was embedded in my being and that to ask for help was to admit my shortcomings. I don't seem to be alone. We often hear "I don't need any help," or "Mind your own business. I can do this by myself."

Self-reliance is, of course, a necessity in adulthood. But carried the extreme, it builds a barrier to necessary friendships, resources, and the practices of mutual help that have defined successful human endeavor for thousands of years.

Our popular image of the self-sufficient pioneers is based on myth more than fact. In practice, whole communities gathered to help build a barn, clear land, defend the community and worship.

In life today, help is only steps away – whether the drug store, our family, the school nurse, friends or professionals. But too often we come to believe that seeking or getting help is a sign of weakness.

People like myself, who see benefit to using mood altering substances, certainly don't want help that will suggest stopping such dependencies.

Getting help itself is not necessarily a "surrender," but more of an admission that we can't get to where we need to go on our own.

It seems easier to admit that help would be useful when we face physical issues: a broken bone, a roof repair, or even losing weight. The tough job is accepting the need for help with things that affect us emotionally: unfruitful relationships, feeling less valuable, fear of unfamiliar situations, or dependence (on people or substances).

For the entire human experience, help from others lets us feel valuable and "belonging." At the same time, feeding our souls with a healthy spiritual relationship is a powerful resource.

I like to think of my spiritual life as a special battery that was installed at birth. For many years, I bragged about my inner strength as my battery was losing its charge. I would not admit that the charge I needed came from a spiritual world – a higher order that (for me) includes connection to all humans before me, my human brothers and sisters of all places and races, and a divine presence composed of this eternal wisdom.

The decision to seek and respond to available friendships and a higher wisdom changes lives. Using these resources through conversation, meditation, and even prayer charges my batteries.

Again, those using the Twelve Steps will see that "getting help" is a reflection of Steps Two and Three.

Tool: **ACCEPTANCE**
Bullet Points:

- *See help as a deserved option, not a mark of failure.*
- *Test drive the spiritual life.*

6.

GET HONEST
The Recovery Journey

Human beings are designed to be motivated by rewards. In either the short term or the long term, we are most successful when we are confident and feel good about ourselves at a fundamental, or internal level.

We have a reward mechanism build into our "primitive" brain, the limbic brain. While brain chemistry is complicated, it is useful to know that dopamine is released as a reward to give the rest of our brain the feelings of success – a natural "feel good" message.

It is a perfectly natural desire to try to shortcut this mechanism.

We can cheat to get to the head of the line, lie to get what our infantile brain demands, trim the truth to beat the competition, or steal things that don't belong to us to satisfy our impulsive demands.

We can also manipulate the brain by introducing chemical "shortcuts" to good feelings – even euphoria. We can do this temporarily. If we pursue manipulation on a regular basis, however, we develop dependence on these mood-altering chemicals. Natural motivations are replaced by chemical ones. There is a name for this: addiction disease.

Dishonesty always comes home to roost. Corrosion of values, reputation and self-esteem goes along with cheating.

But rewards are still vital to growth and life fulfillment. People with addiction disease can change. The beginning of change from artificial rewards to real rewards is by becoming willing to change and putting new emphasis on being ready to change.

That means being ready to live in truth. And to begin believing that lasting rewards are won honestly.

Living in truth is a lifetime journey, but exceedingly rewarding. It is useful to break it down to mini-steps. For instance, Twelve Step programs divide the work into:

- Being true to ourselves by becoming more self-aware of our assets as well as our shortcomings. (Steps Four and Five)
- Being true to your spiritual foundation, or God, if you please. (Steps Six and Seven)
- Being true to others – restoring and using relationships with family, community, associates, the human family. (Steps Eight and Nine)

Tool: **TRUTH**
Bullet Points:

- *See how dishonestly comes home to roost.*
- *Lasting rewards are won honestly*
- *Be true.*

7.

GET CONNECTED
The Recovery Journey

Isolation is a primary symptom of active addiction disease. Even though we often begin using alcohol and other drugs as a social lubricant, in time we find ourselves alone – even in a crowd.

This characteristic often reinforces the idea that people with an addiction problem are inferior in some way, and usually morally deficient. This misunderstanding of the disease concept of substance use disorder is a primary reason why so many people never get appropriate health care for their illness. (Research shows that less than ten percent of people with an addiction diagnosis get treatment.)

Healthy people build relationships in their lives that allow them to process their experiences, their learning, and their hopes with other healthy people. It is by sharing that we remain healthy.

Lack of sharing leaves us stagnant, depending on our thinking to process decisions. The decisions we make in isolation are not usually the best ones. For people on a recovery journey, connection to others is critical. Here are a few suggestions for connecting that can bring mutual support, fresh perspectives, and a fuller, happier life.

- **Be open.** Place yourself in circumstances where like-minded people are likely to be. Recovery meetings let us hear each other and test whether a relationship is useful. Be positive and assume people are trustworthy until proven otherwise. Lots of people in early recovery start realizing that they have been closed off to others for a long time. When they start listening, they find people at work and associates (even at home) that are well worth hearing. Starting with a sponsor who has experience on the recovery road is a good first step.
- **Be choosy.** You can be friendly with everyone, but make choices on the level of trust and sharing. Many find that a good mix is important to well-rounded living. For many, it is important to keep associations with people of like culture or similar origin. But also reach out to people of other backgrounds, faiths, professions or ages. Also, it is perfectly natural to move on when an association is not benefiting either party.
- **Be consistent.** Dependability is a mark of trustworthiness. If you expect that of others, display it in yourself. If a particular relationship is beneficial to you, invest in it with your time and your attention. "Showing up" for life is a new experience for many in early recovery. And it proves to be helpful in finding and keeping friends.
- **Be grateful.** I know today that teachers were in my life from the beginning. I simply wasn't paying attention. Today, I am open to others

as well as myself. And I find teachers almost every time I am in need of help, comfort, instruction, or just a kind word. And once in a while, I serve as a teacher for someone else. For this I am grateful.

These are the lessons of Steps Ten, Eleven and Twelve.

Tool: **HEALTHY FRIENDS**
Bullet Points:

- *Place yourself with like-minded and like-motivated people.*
- *Move on when an association fails to benefit.*
- *Notice and be grateful for teachers.*

8.

THE SERVICE PARADOX

One of the most peculiar paradoxes is the idea that serving others benefits ourselves. Whether following Rotary Club International's call for "Service Over Self," Christianity's example of Jesus' journey, or the Twelve Step tradition of "carrying a message," people in all walks of life have found solace, peace and practical benefits by focusing on helping other people on their journeys.

Why and how does this work?

On one hand, it is argued that self-care is essential for good health and good relationships in society. Exercise, vitamins, meditation, education, and many other strategies help us with self-care.

Yet another argument says, on the other hand, that "getting outside of ourselves" is a healthy path for emotional peace and health. This suggests that too much self-focus contributes to physical illness. It is important to recognize that taking care of the business of life is both an intellectual and an emotional effort.

Beyond the logical arguments, we have the evidence of the human race throughout time. Those who achieve the most in peace and fulfillment always seem to be the ones who devote significant time and energy to the needs of others. It isn't just Jesus of Nazareth or St. Francis of Assisi who demonstrate the value of service. It works for everyone and anyone who tries.

Muhammad Ali is quoted as saying: "Service to others is the rent you pay for your room here on earth."

Practicing service need not be difficult or complex. I have a friend who finds renewal at the end of the day being the unofficial greeter at recovery meetings. "I elect myself to the greeter position and shake hands with everyone entering the building," he says. "Then I go in, sit down, and enjoy the fact that all the hassles of the day have disappeared from my mind."

The release valve for our emotional health is relationships with other human beings. Our need to have connection is built into our DNA. Failure to engage with others brings personal growth to a halt.

Looking at life through the eyes of another, while being of real and practical help to that person, brings not only growth, but also joy.

My service began by setting up chairs and making coffee for recovery meetings. Over the years, I have maintained my service at recovery meetings, including helping start two recovery clubs. But I have also been called to outreach: Taking recovery meetings to jails, testifying before lawmakers about addiction health policies, and helping organize a national movement of people in recovery.

In whatever way service to others is practiced, the engagement is healing. And the benefits are real.

Tool: **SERVICE**
Bullet Points:

- *View the world through the eyes of others.*
- *Realize your own gifts for service.*
- *Make service a daily habit as well as an occasional special treat.*

9.

Nothing to Hide

Junk has become a major business in many communities. We cling to things that don't apply to our current lifestyle, but hold so many memories that we hesitate to call them "junk" or throw them away – even when they could be recycled for others to enjoy.

As our society becomes more mobile, moves from one home to another become milestones in our lives. Each move involves emotional as well as physical transfers.

Sorting out "valuables" from the "formerly valuable" brings back memories and emotions – both happy and sad. In fact, moving is considered one of life's major emotional challenges.

Emotional junk is often hazardous to our health, especially for people in addiction recovery. And so much is hidden from view. Much that we think is hidden is actually well known by our family, friends and associates.

Most of the hard work in a recovery journey involves identifying hidden and painful memories that have not been processed appropriately. Inventories, as well as sharing with sponsors and professionals, free us from past shame fears and open us to living in transparency and joy.

When we are free of these "ghosts," we are open to daily joys we never imagined.

There are things that should be "confidential," of course. Like passwords.

But waking up to life with nothing to hide is truly transformative. By dealing in the present, you have more energy to overcome challenges. And staying in the present with a clean slate is an awesome way to meet and greet people that cross your path.

Tool: **SORTING**
Bullet Points:

- *Find what's valuable today.*
- *Identify junk on a regular basis.*
- *Enjoy a clean slate.*

10.

BUILDING TRUST

Trust is the pavement of a happy and productive life journey. Trust is the result of reliable behavior. There is a saying that we lose trust by the bucket and earn it by the thimble.

Few people enter recovery with pristine stories of reliability, faithfulness and attention to duty. Yet the often painful rebuilding of trust furnishes a foundation for a "life beyond our wildest dreams."

We cannot *talk* our way into trust. It is earned one step at a time through our *walk*.

Our disappointing performances have separated us from others over time. We have lost connection – that necessary bonding that is required by our innermost spirit. As others lose faith in us, we lose faith in ourselves.

And too often we react to these very real barriers with misunderstanding and anger. The consequence is more erosion of trust, and further distance from those we need the most.

"How dare you ignore my feelings," we say. "Can't you see I am sober!"

We demand attention. We expect forgiveness. We want respect and acceptance – though completely on our terms.

But we are the person we trust the least. The inventory process in Twelve Step programs teaches us to start by facing ourselves. And forgiving ourselves. Before we can heal the resentments of others, we must heal the pain and disappointment within us.

Digging deep, seeking truth, forgiving ourselves, changing our goals, learning new practices, and finding peace: These are the mini-steps to building trust.

Achievements last in direct proportion to the time we spend in preparation. This is true in building a skyscraper or a rewarding life. People who invest in their personal honesty are doing foundational work.

We must make reasonable attempts to make amends and restore trust. But not just for the object of getting the acceptance by others, rather to develop acceptance of ourselves.

Doing the inside work prepares us for a life of happiness and maximum service to others.

*Tool: **EARNING TRUST***
Bullet Points:

- *Stop living to impress others.*
- *Reclaim our intrinsic value.*
- *Celebrate the healing.*

11.

CHECK YOUR MOTIVES

How sweet to find shortcuts to life's rewards. Or so it seems. Our rationalization tells us we get to "the head of the line" because we deserve it, no matter the damage to others. Our brain loves pampering and is happy to furnish artful justifications.

Life, however, has a way of returning self-centered behavior "in the mail." Our short-sighted efforts often cost us relationships, opportunities, and learning.

For the person in addiction recovery, past experience with "shortcuts" returns as an issue we must process in order to build a solid, long-term foundation of recovery. As we learn to establish better relationships, we are often cautioned: "Check Your Motives."

I am often reminded of the Native America legend about wolves: Everyone houses two wolves in their being, according to the legend. One is the good wolf. The other is the evil wolf. Over our lifetime, only one wolf will survive.

How do we know which wolf survives? The legend's answer is simple: The surviving wolf is the one we feed.

If we feed hate, jealousy, selfishness, and sloth, the evil wolf survives and becomes our persona in this life. If we feed love, joy, faithfulness and care for others, the good wolf survives and becomes our demonstration.

The assumption may be that our motives are questionable. But the fact is that motives are essential elements of growth. Motivation is required for moving forward as well as turning away from life's lessons.

Einstein once said: "Life is like riding a bicycle. In order to keep your balance, you must keep moving."

The same is true of the recovery path. The person motivated to keep on learning and growing never needs to worry about losing balance – or experiencing relapses. Striving for competence, success, peace and happiness enhances our journey. When our motivation is concerned solely with our selfness interests, the journey comes with a few more pot holes.

Tool: **MOTIVES**
Bullet Points:

- *Separate self-centered from life enhancing.*
- *Feed the positive motives.*

12.

THE MEDICAL VIEW

The medical view of addiction sheds new light and hope for an illness that has debased and destroyed lives for centuries. Medical science in the 1990s taught us more about our brains than we had learned since the beginning of civilization. This research clearly outlines altered brain functions that result from misuse of chemicals, as well as malfunctioning internal production of dopamine that throw emotions off balance and encourage misuse.

These findings reinforce Bill Wilson's earlier assertions about addiction as a physical allergy in addition to a mental obsession. AA's early teaching about addiction as an illness – not a moral failure – marked a turning point in assisting wellness and recovery.

Additionally, those experiencing recovery often mark their personal turning point as the moment when they accept that they are sick people needing healing, not bad people needing punishment.

Understanding the health implications of addiction opens many doors to healing. The healing tools for addiction health include:

- A correct view of life's difficulties.
- Processing, through guided group therapies, the thinking, feeling and behavior patterns of a lifetime.
- Right-sizing the ego.
- Medications, in some instances, that block harmful chemicals from acting on the brain, or reduce cravings for harmful substances.
- Connection with a supportive community.
- Time.
- Gratitude.

It is also useful to realize that many people with addiction illness have other health concerns. Up to 70% of individuals diagnosed with addiction disorders have additional behavioral health conditions – most often depression and anxiety.

Behavioral health science has underscored the need to address all these issues at the same time. Competent professional help is vital and can include individual counseling, outpatient care, residential care, and support groups such as Twelve Step fellowships.

Happily, the science of addiction health has advanced significantly in recent years. Appropriately trained physicians, psychologists, counselors and treatment providers are more abundant. And commercial insurers are beginning to cover addiction health.

Tool: **SCIENCE**
Bullet Points:

- *Accept medical view of addiction disease..*
- *Address whole health concerns as part of full recovery.*

13.

A Cup of Zest

It is useful for many on the recovery journey to envision our hearts as a cup. Each day begins with the cup being empty. As we wake, the cup immediately collects our thoughts and feelings and quickly fills to the brim.

As we engage the day, we hit the inevitable bumps – contacts with family, co-workers, clerks, teachers, students, neighbors and more. With each bump, whatever is in our cup spills and sprays on the people we meet.

Without even thinking about it, we can spray positive or negative feelings on our relationships – be they spouses or gas station attendants. And often what we spill defines us to others.

Picture a person obsessed and angry over how they were treated the previous day. Or fearful because of an embarrassing moment they cannot seem to forget. This person's negative feelings, unprocessed, leave a trail of messy and unsatisfactory engagements throughout the day.

Neither that person, nor anyone he or she meets along the way are very happy about bumping into one another.

There is little to encourage positive conversation or to find enjoyment in the encounter.

Unfortunately, this is the rule for people who dwell on negative experiences and issues without "cleaning house" for a new day. Without a discipline to focus on the positive, our mind fills the heart cup with negative ammunition for the coming day.

The best "house cleaning" discipline is gratitude. By starting each day with a gratitude list, today's cup begins with positive thoughts, uplifting goals, and a smile to welcome each encounter of the new day. Each "bump" spills love, joy and a zest for life.

It is useful to tap spiritual strengths and practices. Meditation is a proven house cleaning tool.

The people we encounter respond to positive spills. The possibilities of the day move to the foreground and take a different shape – even when facing difficult challenges. Opportunities emerge from difficulties throughout life. Look for the lemonade.

Tool: **HOUSE CLEANING**
Bullet Points:

- *Our cup stays full, but can choose positive energy over negative.*
- *Others "read" our energy.*
- *Look for the lemonade.*

14.

Resentments R Us

Resentments are of marginal value to anyone, but are sure threats to anyone in addiction recovery. The beginning of any relapse is usually a resentment.

Whether we are slighted, or significantly damaged by the behavior of others, our internal judgment seeks justice. Our feelings are hurt and we believe we won't have peace until someone is brought to justice.

Worse, our own behavior is altered by the weight of carrying such baggage, even if we try to keep our resentments a secret.

There is an African saying that describes what happens:

"When you don't talk about something, that something will talk about itself for you."

And resentments talk loudly – even if you don't say a word.

Negative reactions to people or situations can range from disappointment to anger. Training one's self to pause, take a deep breath, and figure out appropriate responses is hard work. With some work and time, it is possible to think first and act second. A one-word prayer can be useful: "Help." Your Higher Power is listening.

Practice separating disappointments from resentments. Disappointments can be discussed – carefully. Resentments have to be set aside. We have to own up to the fact that we are not the judge or jury for the world. And even if our position is "right," we are in no position to police other people, particularly those who don't agree with us – or those who would do us harm.

It helps to remember that our demands for justice are rather ironic in light of our history of avoiding life through alcohol and other drugs. "Letting go" gets easier with practice.

Tool: *FLAG RESENTMENTS*
Bullet Points:

- *Separate disappointments from life resentments.*
- *See relationships and conflicts in appropriate context.*
- *Practice "letting go".*

15.

FREEDOM TO ENGAGE

Living life on a spiritual wavelength is liberating. With no secrets to hide, no resentments to parade, and nothing to prove, we can be free to face life on life's terms. And that includes being open to others – at all times.

Transparency, something we used to fear, can, in fact, be joyful and very fruitful. Author Brene Brown discusses joy in being vulnerable: "Courage starts with showing up and letting ourselves be seen. Through my research, I found that vulnerability is the glue that holds relationships together. It's the magic sauce."

This does not mean that everyone we engage with becomes our best friend. But it opens possibilities for relationships beyond our best planning or wildest dreams.

Twelve Step literature suggests that when the pupil is ready the teacher will appear. Most of us realize how many potential teachers we either passed up or pushed away during our using experience. Today, teachers, friends, confidants and other examples of spiritual living accompany our journey if we allow it.

Listen today for a fresh voice of encouragement. Watch along your path for opportunities to share – and help.

A person with more time on the journey than I told me a sure cure for the blues:

"Appoint yourself the greeter at any meeting. Welcome folks with a smile and a hug. Before long you will find yourself in the best mood of the day."

Tool: **TRANSPERENCY**
Take Aways:

- *Recruit teachers.*
- *Enjoy your place in the human race.*

16.

THE WISDOM TO KNOW THE DIFFERENCE

Spiritual living is available to everyone, free of charge and without obligations. Think of entering a pasture, a place of spiritual nourishment without a fence, open to all, with abundance shared by all.

But also see how people access this abundance from their own perspectives, establishing "gates" around the meadow: the Baptist gate, the Catholic gate, the Buddhist gate, and so on. People passing through these gates enjoy the nourishment as much as those who avoid the gates.

It does not diminish the benefits of organized religion to understand a Higher Power as the host of eternal wisdom who meets and dispenses that wisdom individually – as needed and as requested.

A friend of mine goes so far as to say, "we are all spiritual beings, currently enjoying a human experience."

Carl Jung's writings reflect a suggestion made by others that eternal wisdom is composed of the experiences of all those who have "gone before us." Our own inner spirit and voice benefits from a conscious contact with this wisdom source.

The proof is in the pudding, as they say. Those who regularly practice the Serenity Prayer have little doubt that wisdom is there when needed. First, practice acceptance. Second, identify the things you can change and get busy. Third, seek and find the inner voice of wisdom.

Remember that you are not in charge of the wisdom. It will not appear at your command. But with patience and a little humility, it will always appear. In God's time, as we say.

Tool: **FAITH**
Bullet Points:

- *Practice prayer and meditation.*
- *Accept limitless wisdom.*

17.

WHEN "BAD" THINGS HAPPEN

People in addiction recovery often say "I do not have problems today, only situations. It's only a problem if I pick up a drink or drug."

Life does present difficulties. At first glance these challenges can appear threatening. These times test our spiritual condition. When we are grounded in our faith and are "growing along spiritual lines," we calm our emotional reactions, plan options with patience and good guidance, and then act with trust that all things will turn out for the best.

"What nonsense!" you might say. But the evidence is pretty clear. When we act with truth, confidence and trust, the direst situations often turn out to be growth experiences and even blessings.

Especially ticklish are the situations created by our own ego getting in our way. It is tough to see, much less admit, that some of the garbage is on our side of the street. This is where healthy support networks are invaluable. Having people in our life who share our disease and recovery path is a tremendous asset in tough times and situations.

When situations appear, we have a proven process:

- First, take an honest inventory.
- Second, seek others' experiences and points of view.
- Third, operate with patience and love for all.
- Fourth, be grateful for recovery.

Tool: **SITUATIONS**
Bullet Points:

- *Calm our emotions.*
- *Plan options.*
- *Know that "all is well."*

18.

BUILDING RELATIONSHIPS

Traditional views on marriage vary widely around the world. Many cultures feature arranged marriages where mates are selected or negotiated by parents. In the United States, by and large, dating and negotiations directly between potential husbands and wives is featured.

This pre-supposes that long lasting love in a relationship is experienced more often when individuals select their "one true love" as opposed to when they meet each other at the marriage ceremony. The assumption is that searching for and finding a perfect mate is the ideal strategy for marital happiness.

However, what is clear through research is that lasting relationships depend much more on "doing the work" than on simply seeking the "perfect" partner. The same is true of all relationships – business, family, school and social friendships. In each of these linkages, the benefits go to those who jointly invest in the relationship through caring, listening, and sharing experiences, strengths and hopes.

Many of us come into addiction recovery grieving badly shattered, or lost relationships at every level. The consequences and costs of our misuse of mood changing substances are exacting and go way beyond financial considerations.

It may be possible to sweep aside the past, start fresh in building friendships, and create a new life while ignoring past wreckage. But it doesn't usually work very well. For one thing, we still bring our old selves into new relationships. As is said: "Wherever I go, their I am." It is no wonder, then, why we get mixed results even though we are not drinking or drugging.

Over time, it has proven a lot more beneficial to improve the "old self" – learning new skills, adopting new attitudes, and gaining insight into what are surface impressions and truly valuable exchanges. We learn this by facing our histories, confronting our mistakes, and doing our best to build a "new self."

Some see value in an "amends" process, seeking to set things right with people we have harmed in some way. And there is some value in repairing past damages. The real progress, however, is in looking at "amends" another way. The true definition of "amend" is "to change."

Many of us coped with life while practicing our addictions through solitude. In fact, isolation is considered a primary symptom of addiction disease. Even with many years of recovery, a sudden impulse to isolate remains an active symptom.

Experience teaches us that relationships are not only valuable for improving the quality of our lives, but is particularly helpful for staying free of alcohol and other addicting substances. Here are a few tips on establishing and maintaining healthy relationships:

- Be willing to recognize and meet people with something to share.
- Understand that when we become teachable, teachers will appear.
- Never enter a relationship with a self-serving agenda.
- Pursue your passion and welcome those who join you along the way.
- "Honesty is the only policy" when it comes to relationships.
- Never assume others can see your gratitude. Say it often.
- Be open to feeling the "spirit" in a relationship, not just the words or even the actions.
- Value your successful relationships more than gold.

Tool: **DOING THE WORK**
Bullet Points:

- *Recognize what did not work in the past – and amend (change) behavior.*
- *Beware of isolation.*
- *Value your growing relationships.*

19.

SAY THE SECOND THING...

We learned more about brain science in the 1990s than in the total era of all our previous knowledge. The health industry is (sometimes slowly) integrating this knowledge into practice. These findings have the potential to dramatically change our understanding and advance our opportunities for healing and satisfying lives.

Much of our previous view on human behavior was excellently constructed by B.F. Skinner in the 1960's and 70's. Skinner described the "technology of behavior" in very specific terms and made the case that humans recognize and pursue their best interests and act accordingly – motivated by life's rewards and punishments as they are applied to each person.

Little space was left in this theory for competing interests of cognition-informed vs. spirit-informed views within each individual.

More recent evidence indicates that our brains have great capacity to react emotionally as well as practically to most situations. Hence the SECOND THING THAT COMES INTO YOUR MIND!

Our first view of new information is nearly always reflective of our fears and/or hopes. Most people are prone to overreact in direct proportion to the power of that fear or hope within them.

Our "second view" processes the new information through our cognitive brain, the frontal lobe that considers the wisdom of past experience and is capable of projecting consequences of our responses and behaviors.

Many of us come to regret our inappropriate first responses. Often, our emotions and feelings are speaking. Our self-centered fear demands a strong, if inappropriate, defense.

Waiting for the "second thing" to emerge from our thinking is particularly good advice for people in addiction recovery. We have harbored so many resentments and fears over the years that it takes some time to respond from a place of gratitude and wisdom.

Yet even as we benefit in daily communication by "saying the SECOND THING," we cannot ignore the issues in our lives that prompt the habitual "FIRST THING". Negative "first things" are often clues that point to work yet to be done to overcome resentments, bad moods, even depression.

In time, our SECOND THING can make the best FIRST IMPRESSION – one of joy, love and appreciation for all our brothers and sisters on this planet.

Tool: **PATIENCE**
Bullet Points:

- *Recognize the voice based on emotion.*
- *Wait for the cognitive brain to speak.*
- *Consider how to make the best first impression.*

20.

It's Hard to Hate Up Close

People are in our lives for a purpose. Not that we always understand or appreciate that at first.

Humans have evolved to operate in community. It is interesting to observe that the most vibrant communities in the world are the ones that not only tolerate, but encourage diversity of thought and action.

It often takes a few years of life to understand and appreciate that differences are as important and useful as similarities. In youth, we can't stand to be different from "our" crowd. We seek friendships to avoid challenges. When challenged, we often shrink from the battle.

As we mature, we begin to appreciate opposing views, even when we don't adopt them. We assess our own feelings and thoughts when challenged, perhaps adjusting a point here or there, but inevitably becoming stronger and more satisfied with our views and position.

We learn it is foolish to push away people who disagree with us. This does not mean we need to tolerate rudeness, or encourage those who would harm us. But tolerance and engagement with others are good strategies for life.

Former Vice President Joe Biden, in discussing relations with other societies, cultures, and nations, once said: "It's hard to hate up close." He explained that contact is beneficial, dialogue is fruitful, and seeing is believing.

Technology, in some ways, has not been helpful. The invention of the telephone broadened our ability to connect with others, but diminished the quality of our conversation and understanding. "Voice-only" communication misses much of the context and emotion that is vital to understanding. Today's texting and tweeting emphasizes even more of the rough edges on our sharing, without the nuance or context of our views or feelings.

Finding joy and fulfillment through outreach to others, in our work, travel, or learning takes effort. But the connection builds a better life. As was said by the Michael Corleone in God Father II:

"Keep your friends close. But keep your enemies closer."

Tool: *APPRECIATE DIFFERENCES*
Bullet Points:

- *Learn through challenges.*
- *Dialogue is fruitful.*

21.

WELCOMING CHANGE

As the consequences of practicing addiction grind us down, we become very skilled at rationalization and avoiding responsibility, i.e., the "blame game." All our shortcomings result from someone letting us down or failing us in some way.

As our recovery progresses, our perspective changes and we see taking responsibility a desired behavior that we formerly sought to avoid. This is change taking place in the core of our being. And as we count the days of being sober and clean, and our physical condition improves, we enjoy moments of joy in our daily achievement.

We welcome contact with our family, friends and close associates. And we regret our role in some of the hard times in our past. As we lift our eyes from momentary survival and view the expanded landscape of our lives, past damages due to our behavior emerge as barriers to moving forward. We may fear either rejection or punishment as a consequence of our misuse of alcohol and other drugs.

From hurt feelings and family disappointments, to legal issues or time incarcerated, consequences carry forward in one form or another. They become either situations to manage or insurmountable barriers to the future. The choice is ours.

The work in recovery is to orient ourselves to the present and stay on a recovery path that becomes more familiar each day.

We face the past from the viewpoint of the present and seeing change for the better as a fruitful consequence. The victory, however, is not won by how we mitigate past damage. Success comes from finding ourselves, discovering or restoring our inner values and beliefs, and practicing new behaviors in the present.

If nothing changes on the inside, sooner or later our behavior will continue to disappoint and new damages are added to those of the past.

On the other hand, when we change our orientation and embrace new life, positive changes emerge all around us – even as we tackle some of the tough work of life on life's terms.

A pivotal step on the road to inside change is to answer the question, "Who Am I?" Most of us find we have buried our real identities under a ton of manipulation, targeted to get what we want when we want it – unconsciously pursuing the addiction to "more."

There is no fast track to finding one's self. It is not just a thinking exercise.

What works is developing relationships with others that allow us to share our fears, dump our resentments, talk about what we most value, feel the love around us, and seek a path that lets us forgive ourselves as well as forgiving others.

Many of us emerge from this process learning the benefit of a "conscious contact" with a power outside ourselves – a "higher power" or eternal wisdom. We individually come to an understanding that works for us. New appreciation of our personal values, ethical behavior and increased ties to our individual heritage also describes growth along spiritual lines.

The result is change: change in our view of ourselves and others, and the connectedness possible in lives of service as well as achievement. A lasting result of finding the faith to overcome life's challenges is being rewarded with growth and happiness.

A dear friend in recovery often said:

"Life is all about situations. Situations can always be managed. They only become problems when I find a drink in my hand."

Tool: **CHANGE**
Bullet Points:

- *Recognize what did not work in the past – and amend (change) behavior.*
- *Value your growing relationships.*
- *Nurture your spiritual connection.*

22.

Rewards at Warp Speed

It is a mystery to many people trying to control their drinking or misuse of other drugs to be confronted by how powerless they are over their own behavior. It just makes no sense that we cannot decide to behave one way, then watch our arm pick up a substance and put it in our mouth, nose or arm – in complete disobedience to what our brain just decided.

Welcome to Addiction 101.

Some amazing work occurred in the 1990s in brain science. We learned more about the brain and its functioning during that decade than was known from the beginning of civilization until 1990. Many of our previous understandings or good guesses were confirmed. But this science shed new light on what really occurs in the brains of addicted individuals.

It may surprise most people to learn that alcohol and other drugs do not, in fact, produce the euphoria experienced when we use or misuse these chemicals. They simply activate chemical transmitters in the brain which, in turn, produce the "high," driving the delivering the body's own reward chemicals.

Addiction occurs when outside agents overtake the natural reward systems of the brain and artificially increase the pleasure outcomes. A pioneer in the application of brain-imaging technology to the study of addiction wrote*:

> *"In drug addiction, the value of the drug and drug-related stimuli is enhanced at the expense of other reinforcers. This is a consequence of conditioned learning and of the resetting of reward thresholds as an adaptation to the high levels of stimulation induced by drugs of abuse… during exposure to the drug or drug-related cues, the memory of the expected reward results in over activation of the reward and motivation circuits while decreasing the activity in the cognitive control circuit. This contributes to an inability to inhibit the drive to seek and consume the drug and results in <u>compulsive drug intake.</u>"*

In a more simplified overview, the brain operates with two distinctly different and separate units:

The <u>Limbic Brain</u> is the evolutionary core we share with all mammals. It is responsible for our survival. When we are threatened, this part of the brain takes control, cancelling most other brain functions and focusing exclusively on whatever will ensure our safety, therefore our survival. When you see fire, you run because the limbic brain orders you to run.

The functions of this brain are SURVIVAL, REWARDS, PASSION. This is the source of "cunning, baffling and powerful." When we drink to satisfy thirst, eat to satisfy hunger, mate to satisfy procreation, or run to remove ourselves from danger, we are driven by the limbic brain.

The <u>Cortex Brain</u> furnishes the capacity for THINKING, DECISIONS, REASON, and RATIONALIZING. Through millions of "channels" we either inherit or develop throughout our lives, we obtain, catalog, process and use information and experience to make judgments about the past, present and the future.

In early experiences with drinking and other drug use, our thinking brain can play important decision-making roles. Approximately one in ten individuals, however, lose the ability to discipline their use. An inherited propensity may advance the addiction. Or repeated misuse can overcome existing brain channels and build new ones that reinforce addictive behaviors. In either case, the individual is "rewired" to obey the demands of the reward system (at the expense of the Cortex Brain).

Chemicals vary, as does the way they enter the body, but some can produce pleasure at a rate 100 times more powerful than sexual climax. That is reward at warp speed.

This information is essential to early recovery from addiction illness. The Limbic Brain cannot heal itself. The Cortex (or Thinking) Brain must be engaged in new ways that overcome the survival demands of the Limbic's instinctive brain circuitry. And this process works best when engaged by education, support from others, identifying triggers for use, and planning and executing new behaviors, new associations, and new thinking.

The addicted human brain: insights from imaging studies, Nora D. Volkow, Joanna S. Fowler, and Gene-Jack Wang The Journal of Clinical Investigation | May 2003 | Volume 111 | Number 10

Tool: **KNOWLEDGE**
Bullet Points:

- *Our brains reward actions, especially survival.*
- *Addiction is rooted in the reward center of the brain.*
- *Recovery is built in the cognitive brain.*

23.

LISTENING TO THE
MIRROR'S VOICE

Human beings are thought to be the only life form capable of reflection – an ability to see the past and present in context, and project a vision of the future. Most animals have memories and use them to survive in life. But they have no ability to contextually reflect on life's experiences.

Such reflection is a major asset and is credited with the rapid development of the human race, in creativity as well as wisdom. People in the throes of addiction usually avoid reflection. At best, their reflections are often seriously distorted images, bearing little resemblance to reality.

Restoring a capacity for reflection helps build new pathways during early recovery, a time when we are often still feeling the effects of chemicals in our bodies and learning to think clearly and with perspective again.

It is useful to take time daily and mentally step back from your everyday thinking, and picture yourself in a "mirror of life". Some people close their eyes and begin a quiet meditation, then physically move to a chair across the room to "observe" their thoughts, actions, disappointments and hopes. After viewing these personal aspects objectively, they return to the original chair better composed mentally to meet challenges and enjoy their life.

Another type of self-reflective review addresses life balance, taking characteristics of personhood and scoring whether you are investing too much or too little in each of life's pathways. Here are the aspects of life to review and assess:

INTELLECTUAL – Thoughts, process, perspective, learning and knowledge.

SOCIAL – Relationships, environment, profession, memberships and family.

EMOTIONAL – Mood, feelings, fears and hopes.

PHYSICAL – Diet, exercise, sleep, well-being, body, structure and finances.

SPIRITUAL – Beliefs, values, trust, connectedness, ethics, purpose and prayer and meditation.

In each category, indicate a score: -1, -2 or -3 for an area that is being neglected; +1, +2 or +3 to show that an area is over-emphasized. Saving these charts over time is often a useful chart of personal growth.

Taking care of one's self is a core principle of maturing recovery. Finding balance in the various aspects of life provides the environment needed for a "whole" person to emerge.

A Balanced Life...

Name _____ Date _____

	-3	-2	-1	0	+1	+2	+3	Adjustment Required
Spiritual Health								
Physical Health								
Support Connections								
Work/Learn								
Family/Friends								
Play								
Service								

Tool: **SELF SCORING**
Bullet Points:

- *Observe yourself from across the room.*
- *Ask if you have really found out who you are.*
- *See what is working and how you have benefits.*
- *See what changes would bring your life into better balance.*

24.

FINDING AND NURTURING HOPE

Faith, hope and love. These three attributes are considered by many to be the spiritual cornerstones of life. They are required and are supplied in a fulfilling life. Hope, however, is often the key to reaching that fulfilling and abundant life.

Hopelessness is too often the doorstep for those of us suffering from addiction. We reach that doorstep in disappointment, emptiness and desperation. We have tried every measure of self will to find the solution that alcohol and other drugs once gave us. A symptom of addiction disease is often isolation. We are tired, lonely and hopeless on this doorstep.

Without at least a grain of hope, we are lost. The doorway often leads to seeking another high, avoiding another disaster, blocking out the memories of past consequences, and wrapping ourselves once again in the curtains of shame.

With just a grain of hope, many surrender the dependence on self-will, seek help on another path, and break the mountain of work toward a new life into tiny bits: a day without substances, an hour without regret, a minute without self-disappointment, a second without despair.

We cross the doorstep with that grain of hope, not knowing if things can get better, but just hoping they won't get worse.

Some of us miss the point. We see hope in terms of outcomes. "I hope I pass the test." "I hope I get that promotion." "I hope my mom gets well." "I hope the kids grow up well." "I hope the cop didn't see me." These are wishes for outcome measures to meet our expectations – or (more likely) surpass them.

Hope in the spiritual dimension is not about the past or the future. Not about smoothing the externals of life's journey. It is about living in the present space, reaching deep into ourselves to tap a spring of peace that is realized internally, but has its source in a power outside ourselves. It is a flow that assures us in the present that however the material view looks, that at our core we are valuable, loved, connected to all our sisters and brothers in the human race (past and present), and worthy of the concern and mercy of that Higher Power, we often choose to call God.

The summary judgment of our higher force (regardless of the name we use) is simply: "All is well."

When we live in spiritual hope, the material outcomes may come or go as they wish. But we stay centered and assured that peace is ours – not to earn or to be gifted, but to be claimed and enjoyed.

People in every generation and every spot on the globe have accessed this internal stream, writing of it and worshiping it in innumerable ways. For people in recovery, the discovery and use of this internal resource often seems difficult to claim. After all, we are veterans of self-will, living in either yesterday or tomorrow, and often disconnected from the experiences and supports of others.

We need not be brought to our knees to discover the spiritual path. We do not have to be broken to find hope. But neither should we be surprised if life's difficulties finally force us to look inside ourselves for the light and power to live hopefully – in spite of.

Discovering and using "mystical hope," as some writers call it, is not a one and done assignment. Neither is it about talking the talk. Here are a few proven "walks" on the path of mystical hope.

Listen.

Share.

Be willing.

Be grateful.

Help others.

Repeat.

Tool: **SURRENDER**
Bullet Points:

- *End dependence on self-will.*
- *Break the mountain or work into tiny bits*
- *Stay in the present.*

25.

THE CURRENT OF LOVE

In childhood, adolescence and adulthood, we learn both healthy conditions and situations, as well as unhealthy ones. And we learn how to tell the difference. This self-knowledge includes physical experiences, like knowing one's strength, and emotional experiences, like knowing how to handle rejection. Understanding physical and mental strengths and limitations is particularly useful to people in addiction recovery.

Fortunately, we have a third element of our personhood – our spirit. Most of us with chemical dependence illness know that our physical body and our brain were subject to alcohol poisoning most of the time, preventing any serious ability to seek a new life path in recovery. Addictive substances (particularly alcohol and marijuana) penetrate all body cells on their way to the limbic brain, leaving long-term damage as well as a narrowed capacity to change.

Only the spirit remains free of inebriation. Finally surrendering our will and our body, our spirit provides a window to new behavior first, and new thinking second.

There, deep in our souls, we can connect to reality. In our spirit space, we find the stream of hope that originates from universal wisdom and connects us to eternal truth. It is here that an exchange takes place. It is more than dipping into and claiming our place in the stream of hope. It is receiving in return the signal of belonging we call love.

This exchange happens any time that we are willing. It can, and does occur even when many of our senses are still under the influence of alcohol and other drugs – an influence that tends to remain for days and even weeks after we stop ingesting these chemicals.

Love. Think of it as an electrical current.

It cannot be seen by the human eye. Cannot be packaged, bought or sold. It thrives in the strangest conditions, situations and environments. It flows (like electricity in copper) through particularly friendly conduits to anyplace we are willing to invite it. It is blocked (like electricity facing cement) when we purposely turn away from it.

Its source is common to all. And powerful enough to move each of us when we allow it.

But when the current hits a dead end, the flow stops. We cannot tap into this supply of peace, freedom and validation only to fill our personal needs. When the flow stops, we return to the stagnation of our inner selves.

The opening line of the St. Frances Prayer is the key to spiritual success:

"Lord, make me a channel of thy peace."

To have success with love is simply to be a channel. To let love flow through you to the space and souls around you. This may sound silly and a little woo woo, but try it.

On a personal level, I think of LOVE as an acronym that stands for Lots Of Volunteering Effort – freely given and without expectation. The unconditional love by a parent for a newborn child is a good example.

Practice in meditation a conscious contact with the stream of hope. Accept the flow of love from its universal source. Be open to the humanity around you, sharing (even spilling) your love supply to others. Expect nothing in return except the increase in the flow through you as a channel.

The challenge is to keep the channel free of obstruction, ignore the natural drive to control either the flow or the destination. Return often to the source in your own spirit.

Many have come to believe this universal chain of love continues to expand the nature of humanity into harmony with and tolerance of each other and our core cultures. We see over time an uplifting force that urges universal respect, tolerance and love in the face of fear-driven selfishness, violence and even hate.

For each of us, a wonderful outcome of this discovery and practice is that we begin to love ourselves. To discover our natural place in the human chain. To know we are valued and valuable. To be of service to ourselves and those around us. To be joined to the higher purpose of the universe.

Tool: **SPIRIT**
Bullet Points:

- *Simply be a channel.*
- *The signal of belonging we call love.*
- *Return to the source.*

26.

DRESS FOR THE JOB YOU WANT

Common but useful advice for people entering the workforce is: "Don't dress for the job you have, but dress for the job you want."

The immediate goal of this advice is to pay attention to the clothes you wear and how you present to others. But the larger view is just as appropriate: Wear your internal confidence, your response in language, and your thoughtful manner in a way that reflects your possibility – not just your "getting by" persona.

So, a person in addiction recovery may say: Why are you telling me this? Aren't we supposed to live in the present – not the future?"

Yes. But preparation is today. And the events that shape the future happen in the present. People who present, act, and demonstrate skills, confidence and self-worth get the opportunities. And opportunities, while never predictable, happen in the present.

People in recovery from addiction are also recovering their self-worth. And demonstrating self-worth can be just as useful as demonstrating sobriety. The key to these demonstrations is interfacing with others, not just family and close friends, but circles of people that expand our lives.

These circles include:

- Services – Hair care, regular stores, insurance agents, favorite restaurants, physicians, gym, florist, etc.
- Relationships – Partners, best friends, mentors, teachers, students, golf partners, etc.
- Associates – Co-workers, colleagues in your profession, vendors, consultants, trainers, etc.
- Service – Rotary Club, volunteer work, fund raising, tutoring, recovery group service, etc.

Networking in each of these endeavors builds character and experience that is vital to fulfilled living and happiness. By reaching out to old and new contacts, we build comfort in who we are and how valuable we are. The experience of being open and transparent builds trust in our instincts as well as our higher power. And the reality of networks is that the more we give, the more we receive.

There is a reason that isolation is a primary symptom of addiction disease. The illness likes us to be alone – and needing a drink or drug. Networking is the antidote for isolation.

Networking takes work, however. Just like gardening, contacts and flowers need regular care and watering. For some, a Christmas card is appropriate. But for most, physical contact is vital…a lunch, sharing a meeting, phone calls, and calling on each other for advice and

support is what keeps networks (and you) alive and
healthy.

Tool: *REFLECT YOUR POSSIBILITIES*
Bullet Points:

- *Opportunities happen in the present.*
- *Demonstrate self-worth.*
- *Networking takes care and watering.*

27.

Looking Up to Each Other

⟨⟩

Some years ago, I visited a friend in an addiction treatment facility in a multi-story building. When I signed in as a visitor, I was asked if my friend was on the "alcohol floor" or the "drug floor."

I asked what the difference was and if they had a different treatment regimen for people with different drugs of choice.

"Oh no," was the answer. "Everyone has the same program."

Then why, I asked, did they assign different floors for people with different substance choices.

"I guess everyone has to have someone to look down on," was the impromptu answer.

Dividing people into groups for the purpose of "being better than" has been a human failing over the history of civilization. Even as one person feels abandoned or shamed, that person still finds someone else to abandon or shame. Like revenge-seeking, this practice does not heal and provides only temporary and artificial relief.

It is particularly strange to see this "divide and judge" practice flourish in so-called religious environments. People claiming to follow the teacher who advised "treat others as you would be treated," regularly form isolated, self-righteous groups whose main thrust is to isolate in their judgment of "sinners."

The addiction recovery community is not exempt from such pride and judgment.

But the joy is that a recovery journey both lifts our view of our core value, and gives us the humility to see ourselves as equals among all children of the Earth. We are not "better than" or privileged, nor accepting shame, prejudice or discrimination because of our illness.

In early recovery, it makes practical sense to protect our journey. While being frank and honest with employers and associates, we are careful at the same time to keep our "business" private.

In mature recovery, however, it is a disservice to ourselves to hide our recovery. We have traveled from pleasing others, or being what we had to be to feed our addiction, to knowledge of who we are – authentic, connected, and taking care of business.

This journey to maturity is not instant. It passes through many trials and hardships as well as successes and achievements. We learn to look up to each other, first to people who share our recovery journey, then to people with whom we share space on Earth.

Here is what we do for each other:

- Notice change
- Share experience
- Celebrate success
- Call each other on our stuff

Happy traveling on the Road to Destiny.

Tool: **ATTITUDE**
Bullet Points:

- *Avoid judgements.*
- *Lifts the view of our core value.*
- *Gives us the humility to see ourselves as equals.*

28.

Start with the Body

We bring feelings, fears and hopes into recovery. But all these are housed in our bodies - our life-sustaining factory that more than likely is in ill repair. Our body pays dearly for our "highs," varying with our drug of choice, and repair begins here if the mind and spirit are to have any hope of rebuilding.

Initially, the cells in our bodies join the brain in screaming for "more" when the supply of mood altering chemicals is interrupted. A major part of the detoxification process is getting our cells and organs to return to their assignments.

At some point in the withdrawal, our bodies realize the empty calories of alcohol are not arriving and some repair is in order. The good news is that our bodies know how to repair damages and will redirect energy for the process. That is why we suddenly require significantly more sleep, for instance.

The bad news is that the repair process requires fuel - the fuel usually delivered by a balanced diet. Often we don't get the message and continue to eat sporadically, choosing a mixture of foods that seemed normal while we were still committed to our drug(s) of choice.

The best choice for the first year of recovery is to allow the body to heal itself.

First, set regular times for fuel deliveries: Breakfast, Lunch, Snack, Supper and Snack. Eating small amounts five times a day helps the body-repair project.

Second, write down a balanced general meal plan, getting a good mixture of grains, fruits, vegetables, protein, oils and sweets*.

Third, write down daily what you eat, including quantities, and the times that you eat.

Using a log helps keep your focus on fuel delivery rather than the negative emotions your mind is still trafficking.

Even if you were hospitalized, or in medical care at the time you stopped using alcohol and other drugs, schedule a physical checkup sometime in the first month.

Different substances cause different damage in long term use. Alcohol, for instance, furnishes up to 50 percent of your daily calorie intake – though the calories are not useful for nutrition. Two organs, the liver and the pancreas, suffer significant damage from long term alcohol consumption.

Opiates (heroin, codeine and morphine), which reach the brain more directly, still alter and slow down the gastrointestinal system. Stimulants (crack, cocaine, and methamphetamine) reduce the appetite, causing weight loss and malnutrition. Marijuana stimulates carbohydrate consumption, leading to weight gain.

The mental energy required to learn a little about body repair and proper fuel delivery has the added benefit of taking you away from negative feelings and thoughts.

See HEALING THE ADDICTED BRAIN, by Harold C. Urschel III, MD.

Tool: **REPAIR**
Bullet Points:

- *Schedule physical checkups.*
- *Nutrition provides fuel for repair.*
- *Plan and monitor "fuel" delivery.*

29.

ALLOCATING EFFORT

Life can be compared to a cabinet with several drawers. Placing things in drawers according to their usefulness makes life more efficient and positive outcomes easier to achieve.

I was fortunate early in recovery to have a therapist who taught me useful tools for success. He was a stickler for allocating one's mental energy. One day he said:

"I'd like for you to make a note to post over your computer screen. It should have three lines: AA is for staying sober. Work is to pay your bills. Relationships help you feel better about yourself.

"Your problem," he continued, "seems to be that your desire to feel better about yourself is in the way of other important goals because you demand that outcome from all parts of your life."

He pointed out that since I received significant satisfaction from my recovery community and my job that I was prone to ignore working on relationships. At the time, my marriage suffered significantly from my neglect.

Since then, I have been more careful to look for appropriate results from each of my life's activities.

I learn and practice sober life skills through recovery community connections. But I make sure to take those skills to other parts of life.

I found that my demand that work provide satisfying relationships often came at the cost of making my work profitable. By understanding how to allocate my mental energy, I gave myself a raise over time.

And since I have valued my family, neighbor, and community relationships at a higher level, I have discovered that I value myself at a higher level as well.

The result of this work over time is a better relationship with one's inner self – or "gut," to be more direct. Allocation of effort starts with dividing time more appropriately. But allocation goes much deeper. Since I have sorted and divided my life tasks, I not only set better times aside for each set of activities, I am able to concentrate better on each activity.

Over the years, the once-fleeting thoughts while drinking have become realities:

Regular family gatherings at the beach.

Completing a Master's Degree.

Season tickets to ballgames.

Season tickets to the symphony.

Vacations to distant lands.

Attendance at spiritual retreats.

An appropriate retirement savings plan.

Launching a start-up company.

These benefits grow side by side with regular participation in recovery meetings and events, growing in my business and profession, and much more satisfactory relations with spouse, family and many, many valued friends.

Allocation of effort enhances results in every part of life.

Tool: **PLANNING**
Bullet Points:

- *Allocate mental energy.*
- *Align tasks with desired results.*
- *Allocate time appropriate to whole life goals.*

JOHNNY W. ALLEM
Speaking at the Aquila Awards Dinner at the National Press Club

Allem at the White House with Michael Botticelli,
Director of the Office of Drug Control Policy, in 2016.

Paul Williams, composer, actor, and president of ASCAP
and guest speaker, with Foundation President Johnny Allem.

Allem as a volunteer with Bridges to Communities,
building homes in Masaya, Nicaragua.

30.

THE TWELVE STEP CAMPUS

For more than 80 years, Alcoholics Anonymous has served millions of people around the world in their recovery journey from addiction. It is important to realize both the importance of this contribution as well as the knowledge that we still only serve less than ten percent of the people in need.

Clearly AA is not the only path of recovery. Nor does it replace intensive medical interventions that are often needed. And as science advances our knowledge of brain illness and addictive substances, many find it useful to trivialize the importance of the Twelve-Step model and to attack its principles.

The understanding of addiction illness as both a "physical malady and mental obsession" by the founders of AA was a profound insight more than 80 years ago. This description has been more than validated by the emerging science.

More important than questioning (or squabbling) over spiritual definitions or practices is acknowledging the results these years have demonstrated. The evidence is clear that observing a core practice of AA (and all the other 12-step programs) is useful and healing for millions around the world. This core practice is simply volunteerism – the act of one person helping another with no prospect of personal gain.

Volunteerism is older than civilization. The knowledge that serving the interests of others in fact brings benefit to one's self is at the core of human development. And reimbursing that help with money, goods or honor steals the benefit.

Following this practice is healing and rewarding no matter what banner the work flies under.

Twelve Steps meetings (or campuses) are useful aids to addiction recovery because of this volunteerism, because these self-managed services are ubiquitous around the world, and because they are freely provided. How many mutual aid associations in health management can make such a claim?

This does not mean, of course, that attending AA meetings is the best path for everyone. It does suggest that important coping skills for a recovery life are readily demonstrated by people of all walks of life in these groups. And observing skills at work make it much easier to learn and adapt in the open sharing of Twelve Step groups.

Here are a few suggestions that may help you get the most out of recovery group meetings:

- Attend a meeting at least six times without making a judgment.

- Attend different meetings that may reflect the interests and stories of varied neighborhoods and cultures.
- Always speak to at least two people before or after the meeting.
- Write down suggestions or practices you hear that may be useful.
- Notice how the group responds to newcomers and visitors.
- Be open to new friendships and get phone numbers.

In 1956, AA's co-founder Bill Wilson put this philosophy in the broadest possible perspective:

"Some people think God made life just for happiness, but I find myself unable to share that view. I think He made life for growth and that He permits pain as a touchstone of it all. Happiness – at the very least, satisfaction – is a by-product of really trying to grow. And seasons of real joy are but the occasional product of the process. Which, in eternity, will be the eventual fulfillment.

"Meantime, we seem to be pilgrims on a road – one which you and I are completely confident leads into the arms of God (as we understand Him or Her). If there is no belief in the future life and consciousness, I question if much sense could be made of human existence here. Philosophers can philosophize, and the hearty can beat their breast, but I still don't think the deal adds up to much unless we see ourselves in a Cosmos animated by justice and love. Otherwise, there could be no rhyme or reason to the sort of suffering which you are just undergoing."

Tool: **DISCIPLINE**
Bullet Points:

- *Core practice of volunteerism.*
- *Serving the interests of others in fact brings benefit to one's self.*
- *A Cosmos animated by justice and love.*

31.

ANONYMITY AND TRUST

Anonymous recovery from addiction was a cornerstone of the establishment and growth of Twelve Step mutual aid support. Alcoholics Anonymous was born in an era of moral judgment about excessive drinking and severe consequences as a result of this judgment.

Despite the growth in understanding addiction as an illness and the wider availability of treatment and recovery, the tradition of anonymity continues to benefit individuals on the journey of health and recovery from addiction. There are two principle benefits:

First, while connection to others with similar recovery stories is immensely healing, meetings must be safe places for people to attend and share – particularly beginners on the journey. Sharing must be in confidence. Breaking such confidences can have consequences in the workplace as well as the neighborhood. Gossip is generally harmful and discourteous. Discussing someone else's business or sobriety status is off limits.

Second, an important ingredient of any recovery journey is humility. Many of us bring outsized image of ourselves, often used to cover our inside feelings of low self-worth.

The working definition of humility is to become "right-sized," not better-than, nor less than in the family of the human condition. When our inside view of ourselves matches our outside demonstration, we are on good ground.

Beyond these important benefits are different challenges and opportunities than existed in 1935 when Bill Wilson and Dr. Bob Smith found such sharing to be so beneficial and founded AA. Today, there is broader and more public experience with addiction disease, its consequences and its recovery. One in four families experience addiction up close in one of their members.

No longer is a troubled alcoholic that uncle hidden in the attic. Today's sufferers are younger, suffer in public view, fuel public and private comment, and benefit from wider treatment opportunities and less judgmental prejudice.

This does not mean that negative consequences don't still exist, and too often fall on people in recovery as well as people in active misuse of substances. But there is both greater need and greater value for people with experience on the recovery journey to claim their citizenship responsibilities, carry a message of possibility, and demonstrate for the community that life overcoming challenges is something to be honored and respected.

As we become trustworthy ourselves, it is useful to trust others to respond to truth, change their default judgments, and reduce prejudice. The key to usefulness is to become willing. Once we are willing to demonstrate recovery, appropriate opportunities will occur.

New and old practices of treatment and recovery are rated as "evidence-based." Public policy and public attitudes can also change by examination of the evidence. It is essential to the next generation of people who suffer from addiction to pave the road to health with messages of success and hope. While downside risks still exist, the upside benefits of changing attitudes are significant.

Tool: **A HUMBLE VOICE**
Bullet Points:

- *Connection to stories is healing.*
- *Airing sobriety story of others is off-limits.*
- *The key to usefulness is to become willing.*
- *It is essential to pave the road to health with messages of success and hope.*

32.

CARRYING A MESSAGE

Everyone carries a message. It just may not be the one we desire to share.

When we realize that people see a message in us whenever we pass their way, it behooves us to be sure the message is a positive reflection of our character.

People in recovery from addiction have powerful stories. When delivered with care to appropriate audiences, these stories can save lives, inspire trust, change thinking, and motivate better care for those in need.

The stories grow, however, from the journey – both in practicing addiction and in recovery. And nurturing the story goes hand in hand with nurturing recovery. It is very useful to share these stories in early development with peers along the path. This is healing at work.

But sharing stories outside the treatment or recovery network is another matter. Here are some factors that make stories effective and make it important that people in recovery have a voice and carry a message.

RESULTS – Stories that are helpful to others demonstrate positive results. People starting a recovery journey can demonstrate the pain and confusion of addiction. They can even describe the motivation to change and seek a better path. But only as their journey passes milestones of change can others see a message of hope and achievement.

AUDIENCE – Carrying a message spans a range of opportunities. They include one-on-one conversations, speaking in recovery meetings, presenting in health-related forums, speaking at public events celebrating addiction recovery, and appearing in public media. Each of these venues has challenges as well as opportunities.

ANONYMITY – Stories that help must first assure that they do no harm. Mentioning the recovery status of other people without their permission is not appropriate and possibly harmful. Discussing anonymous recovery meetings or gatherings is also off limits – threatening the safety so important to individuals seeking help at the start of their journeys.

INTEGRITY – Stories of recovery are more than words. Our inside changes shine louder than all the words we can say. There is an authenticity to any story that not only tells the change but reflects it from our inner strength. Such authenticity also is delivered with a humility and gratitude that cannot be manufactured. In short, integrity means that we walk the walk as well as talk the talk.

It is useful to understand that "carrying a message" of recovery is an act of service that benefits the messenger as much as the recipient. And that the actual message is a seed. As a seed, it may not sprout and produce a reaction when the message is received. But may result in action at a critical point in the recipient's experience.

It is also important to realize that messages of experience, strength and hope are uplifting to all of humanity. Our culture is based on stories that are carried from person to person, and generation to generation. It pays to craft our story as we build our recovery.

Tool: **TRUTH**
Bullet Points:

- *Stories can save lives, inspire trust, change thinking.*
- *When a journey passes milestones of change, others can see a message of hope.*
- *Authenticity delivered with humility and gratitude that cannot be manufactured.*

33.

MANAGING CHANGE

The benefits of a life well lived come through change – either seeking change or managing challenges on the journey. The opposite of change is stagnation. There is little or no middle ground.

For people in any stage of addiction illness or wellness, change is a necessary and vital reality. As our disease progresses, for instance, changes occur within and outside of us that are the consequences of our refusal to change.

The changes that occur on our downward spiral include physical deterioration, memory distortion, loss of friends or family, inability to earn a living, loss of faith, and – too often – death.

Changes during recovery include managing our health, building solid relationships, finding better employment, improving home life, getting more education, finding faith and fulfilling service obligations.

Every change – for better or worse – is stressful. Stress depletes energy. Managing change, even when positive benefits are expected, can be difficult. Less stress and better results are possible when steps toward change are understood and allowances are made for time and money resources.

It is helpful to see change as a process instead of an event. Behavioral science has identified the Stages of Change* that help understanding as well as managing the process. These stages include:

PRE-CONTEMPLATION. This is the earliest stage of change, when people are oblivious to a problem, unwilling to address the problem or to consider alternative strategies. We reluctantly move from this stage when circumstances force us, friends suggest the need for change, or professionals prescribe it. Arrests, job or family loss are agents of change on the downward spiral. Job offers, college credits, birth of children, and moving to a new location are examples of change agents on the positive side.

CONTEMPLATION. At this point, an individual takes time to identify the risk and reward factors of the contemplated change. This score-keeping activates the brain in a way that reduces emotional stress while allowing one to assess things in an objective way. Counselors are happy to see someone with an addiction begin to measure the costs and benefits of drinking or using. Even if someone continues to value the benefits of substance misuse highly, they know this process is a significant step toward eventual change. It is not unusual for someone to have one set of values at 7:30 am and another set at 7:30 pm.

PREPARATION. This is the point where we consider taking action about a behavior or a possibility in the near future. We talk to people with similar experiences.

We think about practical changes in schedule or living circumstances. And we plan what steps might be appropriate. Pouring out the last beer at home, or entering treatment might be in this plan. Or visiting a college campus and talking to professional mentors might be a plan for career growth.

ACTION. Success with doing things in a change plan is greatly improved by adequate preparation. Too often we concentrate on people in end-stage addiction illness who are forced into treatment by crisis. And we come to believe that change is a crisis event. It does not have to be. And we do not always have to wait for end-stage illness to get help. People with other illnesses are addressed at early symptoms, and the change process is more objective and less painful. People in recovery also suffer from fear and procrastination when it comes to change. Analyzing costs and benefits, making plans for step-by-step actions, and seeking help and support along the way are all proven tools for successful change.

MAINTENANCE. Sustaining changed behavior can be difficult in any circumstance. It is important to plan ahead and see that a new pathway needs maintenance. In this final stage of change, we work to consolidate the gains from taking action. And we work to avoid slipping back to the earlier state of affairs. If we do stumble (or relapse), all is not lost. We have the commitment. We have the plan. And we have experienced action. We may need to alter the plan slightly, get more support, or renew our faith in our selves.

Those who have traveled this path of change, both in getting well from addiction and enhancing their lives, can testify that even a stumble can be helpful. Every experience we have builds our story. And our stories are about happiness and success. It works for millions.

Understanding change, and applying these proven steps requires work in each level of our being: Our spirit furnishes the passion. Our minds compose the possibilities. Our bodies take us to the action... and success.

DiClemente, 1999; Miller & Rollnick, 1991.

Tool: **CHANGE**
Bullet Points:

- *The opposite of change is stagnation. There is little or no middle ground.*
- *Every change – for better or worse – is stressful.*
- *Change happens in an instant. All the rest is preparation.*
- *Every experience we have builds our story.*

34.

IT'S IN THE AIR

People in my home recovery group often raise their hand high and say "It's in the air!" They are immediately joined with others, showing great smiles and a comradery that demonstrates the unity and comfort of the group. They are demonstrating through this gesture that we are connected and that our sharing not only makes us stronger, but joins us in the greater human spirit.

The idea that our visible bodies and our demonstrated thinking are supported by a spirit force is universal throughout cultures of this world and throughout history.

Carl Jung proposes that there is a permeable membrane between our conscious and our unconscious, permitting exchanges at appropriate times that benefit our lives. He then suggests that another permeable membrane connects us to the universal force where all experiences are homogenized and made available through this higher spirit to guide our journey.

Many people find that nurturing a connection with a spirit force is useful in personal life journeys and especially in overcoming difficulties. Addressing alcoholism specifically has included suggestions about seeking and working with such a "higher power." And the results have been significant for many.

This experience, however, has fueled a major distortion in our understanding of addiction. If spiritual practices are useful in overcoming addiction, it follows for most of society that the difficulty must be a moral one. Centuries of prejudice, stigma and discrimination support the idea that addiction is a moral failure – not a medical illness.

Eighty years ago, the founders of Alcoholics Anonymous got it right. At some stage, we are subject to a physical malady and a mental obsession. And it is often impossible through our will power alone to overcome these disease symptoms.

Using spiritual practices from a variety of traditional sources, AA fashioned a program that has helped millions to recover. This, of course, does not mean a 12-step program is right for everyone, or the only path to wellness. But it affirms that similar practices in meditation and spiritual growth from a variety of cultures that have benefited mankind from the beginning of time.

My friend, Don Coyhis of Colorado Springs, has organized the Wellbriety Movement, tapping the spiritual tools of Native Americans to accomplish results found in Twelve Step programs.

When we practice spiritual tools in any dimension we tap into strength larger that ourselves. This does not negate our individual talents or effort, but enlarges their power and guides our effectiveness. What is essential is that we find our own path. A key to the AA journey, for instance, is "finding a God of our understanding."

As we understand the science of addiction more and more, these traditional paths gain more and more credibility. Today we enjoy other tools, including medications that can reduce craving. But building long-term paths to health as well as lives of achievement and satisfaction are regularly enhanced through spiritual practices.

There are "no wrong doors" to spiritual practice. Here are two suggestions for finding and development a spiritual practice:

First, show up where others are practicing a spiritual or meditation program. Attend four times without making a judgement. Then decide if that practice is valuable to you.

Second, seek practices that both enhance your connection to guidance outside yourself, and build connections that share your journey.

Third, if the first effort is not satisfying, try it a second time.

Tool: **SERENITY**
Bullet Points:

- *Tapping spiritual tools to accomplish results.*
- *We tap into strength larger that ourselves.*
- *There are "no wrong doors" to spiritual practice.*

35.

BECOMING WILLING

Being teachable is not a natural skill.

We come into the world completely self-centered and omnipotent in our own infant minds.

We are told that when a baby is carried into a room full of light, their instinct is to believe they caused the light to come on. The cry of a baby is full-fledged fear at the idea they do not control their surroundings.

Due to various circumstances, we gradually surrender our narcissistic views and learn first to accept and then, hopefully, to seek teachers in our lives. They are there to be found in every realm of life: work, play and relationships. Teachers can guide our physical, mental and spiritual behaviors.

Early life provides specific teachers fulfilling specific roles, including parents, baby-sitters, school teachers, college professors and career mentors. But life provides many more opportunities to learn, usually from those who teach by example.

As life advances, and expectations of competency and mastery increase, many drift toward the view that "I got this." It often becomes a matter of pride to "know" and a humiliation to "ask." This tendency is especially prevalent among people experiencing addiction. As we isolate more and more, we increasingly see ourselves as in control and unilaterally responsible for our well-being. Assistance from others is not only a nuisance, but a threat to our lifestyle.

Recovery often begins with a crisis or intervention that penetrates our isolation. Ideas we never contemplated gradually become acceptable. Examples of others on a recovery journey suddenly have great meaning and we try to adopt their new defenses against taking the first drink or drug.

New possibilities and worthy ideas confront us and we learn from our new "teachers" how to accept change and cope with challenges without misusing substances. As we benefit from new principles of survival and self-care, and develop fulfilling recovery-based lifestyles, we may forget the value of learning and instead become isolated in a new "protected" sanctuary of recovery friends and associates.

Stopping dependence on substances is a major victory. But it should be only the beginning of building a new and rewarding life. Accepting the experience of others (being teachable) is a tool that puts us on a proven path to recovery. But the real rewards come from continuing to live with the tool of being teachable.

Cultivating a life-long practice of learning is both work and joy. First, we must "become willing" by letting go of the idea that we are complete in our knowledge and that learning new things might make life more difficult. But one axiom has benefited everyone who uses it:

"When I become willing, a teacher will appear."

Tool: **WILLINGNESS**
Bullet Points:

- *Teachers are to be found for every aspect of life: work, play and relationships.*
- *Examples of others on a recovery journey have great meaning.*
- *The rule is to "become willing," setting aside the idea that we are already complete in our knowledge.*

36.

A Decision Tool

Life requires decisions. Avoiding decision is in itself a decision to let consequences fall where they will. That is often the history of people afflicted by addiction.

Others often believe we choose to use alcohol and other drugs as though it was a choice between a hamburger or fried eggs. They don't understand the phenomenon of craving in which our brain decides for us to satisfy the body's demand for an artificially induced reward (or high).

Often, when our thinking brain does "decide" to not get high, that decision is high-jacked by our illness.

Our decision-making history, then, leaves much to be desired. In recovery, it takes determination and practice to make decisions and then to act on them. We often start with small successes that grow along with our experience making increasingly accurate judgments and choices in our daily behavior. Gradually, we gain the confidence and experience it requires to make longer range choices – choices that impact our education, jobs and relationships.

Here is a proven tool many have used in early recovery to help make sound choices and decisions:

First, write the nature of the decision across the top of a blank sheet of paper. For instance, "Should I attend my high school reunion next Saturday?"

Second, draw a line down the center of the piece of paper.

Third, write PROS at the top of one column, and CONS at the top of the second column. List the reasons why this is a good idea, and why this is a not-so-good idea in the two columns.

Fourth, after reviewing each of the columns, fold the paper and put it under your pillow for the night.

Fifth, the next day, read the lists again and make an informed decision. It may help to review your work with a sponsor or someone who has experienced a similar decision.

Often we find that by researching potential outcomes and giving the decision some time, our unconscious assists us in evaluating the information and our instinct helps us arrive at a decision.

Sometimes, we find that our instinct (or our unconscious self) has no particular opinion on the matter under consideration. This could be an indication that a decision doesn't need to be made at this time.

Being in touch with our larger spiritual lives is the result of regular attention and work. If we are committed to this work, decision-making often becomes easier. We are more likely to relinquish our demand for instant gratification and therefore, more likely consider longer term benefits and values.

Ideal outcomes are not guaranteed. There is risk to any path. Some of us are more comfortable with risk than others. And, just because an outcome is different than we expect does not necessarily mean we have made a "mistake."

People with a strong spiritual foundations learn that any path can present unexpected, positive opportunities. What appears to be disaster is often just a curve in the pathway of life. If we are willing to learn from our difficult experiences, our future decision-making and behavior will reap benefits.

"Remember, we are always carried," our spiritual advisor may suggest. We only "fall" when we take a drink or drug.

Tool: **DECISION MAKING**
Bullet Points:

- *Our history of decision-making leaves much to be desired.*
- *List reasons why a potential decision is a good idea, and why it's a not-so-good idea.*
- *Be willing to let go of the demand for instant gratification and to give weight to longer term benefits and values.*
- *What appears to be disaster is often just a curve in the pathway of life.*

37.

ADDRESSING CHARACTER

—◦◦◦◦◦—

Our core beliefs and values instruct our lives. They also construct our character. Experiences and information may enhance or alter our beliefs and values over time, but the foundation is usually constructed in early childhood from our earliest teachers, the parents and caregivers who both talk and walk examples of belief and value.

When our actions match our words, we are considered to be strong in character. When our words and actions are inconsistent, our character is considered to be weak.

When circumstances or situations fail to meet our expectations, or challenge our core beliefs, how we respond illustrates the true measures of our character.

Do we defend our values in words and actions without judging others or disrespecting their views?

Do we bend our values in the hope of temporary gain or to save face?

Do we judge and devalue those who upset us or hold different views?

Do we employ anger or revenge in opposing those whose views or actions challenge us?

Many of us see ourselves as strong in character and believe that we carry strong and appropriate messages to others. On closer examination, often during periods of stress or difficulty, we discover issues on "our side of the street" that reveal shortcomings.

The bottom line is that assessing and building character is an act of courage.

The individual in recovery cannot afford to ignore signs of character weakness. Lapses of character can lead to lapses, and eventually relapses, to the use of alcohol or other drugs.

It may be useful to think of our shortcomings as buttons growing on our chest. Buttons that function like doorbells and that others use to get our attention. Children quickly learn how to push their parents' buttons to make demands and to express their views. As adults, we continue to press the buttons of others to try and get the results we want.

Anger, pride, justification, envy, and jealousy are just a few of the buttons most people wear. Once "installed," these buttons cannot be removed. When others press our buttons, we go on the defensive and put the blame game into high gear. Those who would harm or take advantage of us know how, and often, which buttons to push to get what they want.

When engaged in conflict, it is useful to mentally "cut the wires" between your buttons and your mind. Look first to your side of the street, consider the options available to you that are consistent with your core beliefs and life experience, then smile, turn the "other cheek," and proceed about your business.

Cutting the wires behind each button disarms those who would bring us discomfort or harm. It relieves us of the compulsion to respond in kind or consider vengeance. It is also a good reminder that the buttons, though disarmed, don't go away. People will still try them, and it takes consistent vigilance and effort of our part to prevent the wires from growing back.

Living well results from building the highest possible level of character. The more we work on character, the more rewarding life becomes. And the easier to avoid a relapse to our addictive behaviors.

Tool: **COURAGE**
Bullet Points:

- *When our words match our actions, we are strong in character.*
- *Look first to your side of the street.*
- *Working on character leads to a more rewarding life.*

38.

GETTING ON THE SAME PAGE

The family system, whether intact or impaired, is integral to the health outcomes of people experiencing addiction. Two significant factors are often present when a recovery option is presented to someone – by a judge, boss, spouse or someone else:

1. Most likely, the addiction is being addressed in the extreme late stages of the illness. Throughout the progression of addiction disease, literally hundreds of observable symptoms are ignored, even by medical professionals who should know better.
2. There is little understanding of the nature of addiction illness by the individual, family, co-workers and friends. Even when addiction to alcohol and other drugs has impacted the family history, this lack of knowledge leads to responses that make matters worse rather than better.

Most people see the recognition of addiction disease as a verdict rather than a diagnosis. And this underlying misconception makes healing more difficult than it needs to be. Often, everyone involved is on a different page when it comes to recognizing symptoms and – most importantly – building strategies for healing.

Family members are often divided between denying, pacifying and/or punishing the addicted individual. Few recognize that the behavioral aspects of addiction are exceedingly contagious. Outsiders may conclude that the non-using family members are sicker than the using family members.

Here are a few tools that are useful in getting on the same page, building useful strategies, and finding healing for each and every member of the team.

- **Learn about addiction illness.** There is ample reading material in libraries, on-line and through health and social agencies that can provide a foundation of knowledge. A lot or misinformation is also available. Be sure to note the credentials behind information – especially ideas that seem "too good to be true." They usually are.
- **Share the learning process.** Building a team that meets regularly, invites the participation of the addicted individual, seeks professional counsel, and provides unified support for the process and the individual will get results faster – and cheaper.
- **Take individual action.** Each team member can greatly improve the chances for success by practicing individual self-care. This includes demonstrating responsible behavior and establishing/maintaining appropriate boundaries.

- **Re-define love.** Love is not simply attachment. Nor is it using others to fill holes in ourselves. Love matures through difficult journeys. Believe me, this is one of those journeys. The most challenging sacrifice is the giving up of ideas and practices of ours that have not worked. The most successful love can see through the noise and protest that is exhibited during early intervention and stay true to doing the right thing, holding the right responsibility, and showing the right support.
- **Find supporting communication.** Al-Anon and similar organizations offer supportive nurturing and community. Remember that the first meeting you attend may not be right for you. But don't let that convince you that the premise is incorrect. Keep trying until you find the group that works for you.
- **Understand intervention.** There is a point when it is useful to intervene with individuals who have symptoms of harmful health practices or conditions. This is what physicians do during check-ups. The highly staged, confrontational "interventions" associated with addiction illness are sometimes useful, besides making reality television entertainment. More often, sustained interventions by caring family or friends, in concert with health professionals, achieve better and more lasting results.

Learning about family relationships and how they can support recovery is a long-term and rewarding journey. This short essay is but an introduction. A couple of notable assertions are important to remember:

First, truth expressed with love and care are never forgotten. There may be no instant response or recognition, but messages delivered in the family system are never discarded and both positive and negative communications provide vital, life-long impacts.

Second, addiction illness is progressive and fatal. Missed opportunities for intervention and support can be costly. Ignoring evidence and uncomfortable conversations can be dangerous and deadly.

Tool: **TEAM BUILDING**
Bullet Points:

- *Family members are often divided between denying, pacifying and/or punishing the addicted individual.*
- *Love matures through difficult journeys. This is one of those journeys.*
- *Ignoring evidence and uncomfortable conversations can be dangerous and deadly.*
- *Truth expressed with love and care are never forgotten.*

39.

TODAY MATTERS

Today is game day. It is the only time to put points on the board.

When the measure of our lives is totaled, it will be our actions that count. Not our wishes, not our opinions, not our promises, and not our intentions.

When life rolls over on us, bringing challenges or dreams come true, it is our response this day that matters – to our character, our successes or our failures.

In this 24 hours, we can make amends for past actions that were disappointing. We can build on past actions that made opportunities appear today. But no amount of wishing can actually change the past. It is the record. We own it all.

In this 24 hours, we can plan, commit, promise, threaten, prepare for or ignore the future. But the only change on the score board are the actions we take this day.

The importance of "today" is undeniable. Nothing in these words is new. So why do we live in yesterday or tomorrow while the feast of today rots in front of us? Why do we dream of benefits when we fail to do the work? Why do we think today's results will be any different that yesterday's when nothing changes in our behavior.

And why do we feed that compulsion to drink or drug today while saying that tomorrow we will act differently?

The answer is largely that we fear the present. We fear that life will bring us situations that we do not expect or control. We fear that taking actions might be unpleasant. Or that our actions will not work. Or that pain will not go away. Or that we cannot undo past mistakes.

It is not logic that lets us miss the opportunities for action today. We know the truth that today really matters. But our behavior tells a different story. We let our feelings take our minds and hearts to a different place: dreams or fears of yesterday or tomorrow.

So let's start with preparation that comes before any change can take place.

I can prepare for change today by:

1. Meditating for a fresh attitude.
2. Making a plan.
3. Doing the hardest thing first.
4. Making payments on promises: Money and actions.
5. Cultivating relationships.
6. Avoiding hunger, anger, loneliness or being tired.
7. Getting advice.
8. Being open to new people, places and things.
9. Walking, not running.

10. Being grateful.
11. Checking off your plan. Perhaps writing a journal page.
12. Feeding my recovery.

Tool: **TODAY**
Bullet Points:

- *The only change on the score board are the actions we take this day.*
- *Don't let the feast of today rot in front of you.*
- *Start with preparation.*
- *Don't get hungry, angry, lonely or tired.*

40.

ASSIGNMENT: TO "NOTICE"

"I am going to give you a permanent assignment," the therapist told me. I had completed a stint of visits that brought my storied anger into the light and significantly improved my ability to deal with other people.

"The assignment is to notice."

Responding to my puzzled look, he explained that most of us go through life with very narrow parameters for noticing what goes on around us or what people who interact with us are really trying to convey. He went on to list the advantages of noticing.

- Notice, for instance, that we have choices in how we respond to people and situations.
- Notice the affects our words have on others – particularly children.
- Notice when our actions do not match our words.
- Notice when something we said or did a few days or months ago results in benefits or pain today.
- Notice when triggers for old behaviors appear.

- Notice when we make a mistake and the benefit of prompt ownership.
- Notice when others are opening to us in friendship.
- Notice how connections with others benefit us – professionally, socially and spiritually.
- Notice when people need a little assistance and when and how to be helpful.
- Notice you are valuable – to yourself and others.
- And notice the positive things that appear in your life – without your permission.

The job of "noticing" improves with practice. Many find that exercising this coping skill noticeably improves their attitude, peace and joy of living.

Tool: **NOTICING**
Bullet Points:

- *We go through life with very narrow parameters for noticing what people are really trying to convey.*
- *Notice when our actions do not match our words.*
- *Notice the positive things that appear in life – without permission.*

41.

EMBRACING CONSEQUENCES

Consequences have a bad reputation. Our instinct is to avoid them, deny them, or deal with them with dread and sometimes shame. But the fact is that consequences are the proof of life – positive and negative.

A college degree is the consequence of study.

A ticket is the consequence of parking in a no parking zone.

A delicious cake is the consequence of following a proven recipe.

Foreclosure is the consequence of not making mortgage payments.

Multiplied consequences have long-term significance on our lives and the lives of our partners and loved ones. We can learn from consequences and become stronger, better engaged, and more skilled in dealing with life. Or we can avoid the lessons, fail to change our behavior, and repeat again and again the actions that fail to give us the satisfactions we desire.

Those of us who seem to enjoy "learning the hard way" often dwell on feelings. We enjoy good feelings when consequences are good and bad feelings when consequences are less than desirable. But nothing changes when we dwell on feelings or thoughts.

It is our action (or lack of action) that produces consequences. And how we process negative consequences is a major indicator of life success. Here are five tools that are useful in growing from and even welcoming negative consequences:

First, we must own the consequence. This is true even if the consequence is undeserved. Blaming a situation or others for our circumstances fails to move us to another outcome. Throwing the parking ticket in the trash is not a useful strategy, even when we know the parking meter is broken.

More difficult is owning the consequences of our thoughtless, selfish or miscalculated actions. Owning the consequence includes recognizing the harm involved and taking responsibility for the results.

Second, we contemplate our goals – or lack of goals. What alternative actions might change our consequences for the better? What opportunities have we passed over? How does this consequence relate to all the other current outcomes in life? How often do we simply drift through daily life following surface feelings rather than planning and working for specific improvements or goals?

In this contemplation, it is useful to both identify long-term opportunities and goals, and the step-by-step actions that are required to change for the better.

Third, we determine – and write down – a strategy for success. Seeking knowledge and advice from others helps. This plan for better outcomes will change with time and opportunity. But the best results start with a plan.

Fourth, take actions that are consistent with your strategy and plan for change. Each day, list the actions that will advance the plan for improved consequences. Check off the items as the actions are performed. Each action moves the ball down the field. Don't be disappointed if you don't get big scores immediately.

Fifth, practice resilience. The behavior changes because we change. This inner strength to stay the course keeps us committed to action. And our feelings and attitudes benefit from our resilience. It does not have to be painful to grow. Each small achievement builds a competent, fulfilling and joyful life.

Embracing consequences paves the way to successful living.

I love what Mahatma Gandhi said about action:

> "It's the action, not the fruit of the action, that's important. You have to do the right thing. It may not be in your power, may not be in your time, that there'll be any fruit. You may never know what results come from your action. But if you do nothing, there will be no result."

Tool: **ACCOUNTABILITY**
Bullet Points:

- *Consequences are the proof of life – positive and negative.*
- *Nothing changes when we dwell on feelings or thoughts.*
- *Practice resilience.*

42.

WHAT IS YOUR SERVICE POSITION?

It has been my privilege over the years to sponsor people in early stages of recovery from addiction. Depending on their place on the recovery journey they stay in contact with me through a phone call, coffee visit, quick visits at a recovery meeting, or a specially arranged time to work on specific recovery principles.

I usually begin each conversation with a question. It is not a question about having a drink or drug since our last contact. Or about how many meetings have been attended. It is always:

"What is your service position?"

This is a practice I learned from a sponsor when I was new on this journey. From the earliest pain, withdrawal, and adjustment to life without alcohol, to my full and joyful life today, the most useful indicator of success is my service involvement. I have found that this principle is a hallmark of life outside the addiction recovery process as well.

The first feature I take from this question, then, is that service is the best evidence of my recovery health. If

I regularly and systematically accept an assignment to focus on others, I am more likely to keep my life in perspective and find the nourishment I need from others to discern God's will for me this day.

The second feature of this question is the variety of answers it can furnish. Service occurs in many forms and venues. The recovery community and the worship community each have many established service positions for volunteers called to action. Accepting a service assignment not only fulfills a goal to share with others, it fosters responsibility, discipline, and commitment.

Much of service is mechanics. Opening the room, assembling the materials, keeping refreshments on hand, arranging for presenters, keeping records, setting up chairs, and so on may not seem spiritual. But to veterans on the journey, these services promote both healing and humility.

But service is not limited to such organized activities. My first sponsor had a prescription for "hard times." These times were defined by temptation, uncertainty, confusion, hard feelings, or just difficulty paying bills.

"Elect yourself to the greeter position," she would say. "Get to a meeting early, dress neatly, put on your best smile, and say hello to everyone that comes to the door."

This has always been good "medicine" for me. It doesn't take the place of a scheduled service position, but it moves me out of myself and the messy and self-centered thinking that gave me the blues.

Often a leader finds it difficult to delegate or share the service wealth. Too often we believe that it is easier to "do it myself," than to recruit, train, and allow someone new to serve. Nothing could be farther from the truth.

To share the service is to share and grow the team's benefits to all. It is not too much to keep this question on a plaque in our mind's eye – or even on the wall. Each day, each project, each person in our lives can profit from addressing the question:

"What is my service position?"

Tool: **SERVICE**
Bullet Point:

- *The most useful indicator of success is a service involvement.*
- *A service assignment fosters responsibility, discipline, and commitment.*
- *Sharing service is sharing and growing the team's benefits to all.*

43.

Principles Over Personalities

The admonishment to place principles ahead of personalities in our conduct is a standard in the addiction recovery world, stemming back to the earliest Bill Wilson writings for Alcoholics Anonymous.

Placing a priority on principles – like trust, faith, honesty, self-worth – makes common sense. And allowing people to be who they are – whether or not we approve – is a much safer and sensible approach to dealing with life on a day to day basis. Without losing our cool!

Most people find these ideas useful. Digging a little deeper, however, into the roles of principles and personalities gives us further understanding on how these roles are so difficult for people experiencing addiction.

The first thing to note is how we sought and reinforced isolation – that poisoning practice so much a part of our illness.

We watched ourselves betray the principles we learned in childhood. We did not lie, steal or break trust because we did not know better. We watched as our addicted brain directed behavior to feed our craving. We nursed our guilt into isolation. We made every attempt to ignore the contempt of others. But we could not escape ourselves.

At the same time, our view of others often looked like a stand-off: I will hate you before you hate me. Many of us entered our addiction before learning the basics of getting along with others. If we had skills for inter-personal relations, we soon abandoned them trying to defend our misuse of substances. Again, isolation seemed to be our friend.

So, I have stopped using. I feel naked in the world. What do I do?

Somebody says: "Put principles above personalities."

Do what???

Yes, begin with mini-steps to act on the basis of principles. Build trust with one person. Open up and share your feelings once in a while – with no expectations. Slowly we learn that talking is alright, but acting is the real deal. We become honest even when no one is watching.

Remembering, or adopting, core beliefs about the possibilities of life is the foundation of self-esteem and self-value. Living by those principles brings benefits we never dreamed possible.

Then our eyes open to our fellow travelers on the planet Earth. They may think like us, or not. They might like our company, or not. They might look like us, or not. With a little practice, I can listen without judging. I can learn without bragging. I can care without prejudice.

Principles and personalities are important to a recovery journey. Let them grow in value and let us benefit from both.

Tool: **PRINCIPLES**
Bullet Points:

- *Allowing people to be who they are.*
- *Try trusting one other person.*
- *Become honest even when no one is watching.*
- *Listen without judging.*

44.

STAYING TEACHABLE

"Life is difficult." So began Dr. Scott Peck's journey on the "Road Less Traveled" 25 years ago. He led many to focus on the things we can change as opposed to the things we cannot change.

It is perfectly natural, particularly for people in early recovery, to view life's bumps as obstacles. Anything between me and what I want is an unfair, intrusive barrier to my life.

What we often don't want to hear is that life's bumps are opportunities for growth, lessons on living, and blessings in disguise. But seeing these obstacles as lessons and step forward of a journey of achievement is exactly the healthy and productive view.

This view helps us "stay teachable." And staying teachable is one of the most useful tools of successful recovery.

Teachers are everywhere. They show up when you need them the most. But we often do not recognize them. Looking over my history, I can now see how many times people where available to me along life's path, but with my own insistence that "I got this," I simply missed or "blew off" the teacher.

I often watch people emerge from the subway to see the interaction of strangers. Many times, people who are clearly local see confused tourists and ask them if they need directions. After help is exchanged, there is always smiles all around – perfect strangers feeling joy at both giving and receiving help.

Overtime, people in successful, long-term recovery stay open to others, even vulnerable, and always teachable.

First, we remember that our faith has worked. We know that success and happiness are probable in our lives if and when we put trust and action ahead of demands and hopelessness. Faith and trust are the foundations of our recovery.

Second, we stay willing to accept guidance and help.

Third, we observe those who cross our path who have been through a particular life experience. When such friends are not immediately found, we seek a teacher in our network or through professional help.

Fourth, we act on the "teachable moment" to see options and steps which were either not obvious before, or we had passed over through lack of knowledge.

Fifth, we learn our experience may not be exactly as expected, but that surprise endings are usually more beneficial than we planned and always successful in teaching us new lessons.

So, exactly how does that work.

The "joy of living" as described in the Twelve Step programs, is not that we always get our way, but that we advance our level of service to ourselves and others, on the practical as well as spiritual plain.

Then comes the magic moment when someone else finds you useful as a teacher.

Wow…. What a concept!

Tool: **KNOWLEDGE**
Bullet Points:

- *Notice that teachers are available when we are willing to learn.*
- *Asking for help or advice is not life-threatening.*
- *Be open to surprise benefits.*
- *Sharing experiences with others is an act of growth.*

45.

BUILDING FROM THE INSIDE

As the consequences of practicing addiction grind us down, we become skilled at the blame game. All our shortcomings are because someone else let us down. Or failed us in some way. We become very skilled at rationalization and avoiding responsibility.

Entering recovery, we begin to identify our role differently and see taking responsibility as an adult behavior we have managed to avoid. In short, change takes place in the core of our being. And as we count the days of being sober and clean, and our physical condition improves, we enjoy a moment of joy in our daily achievement.

We welcome contact with our family, friends and close associates. And we regret our role in some of the hard times in our past. As we lift our eyes from momentary survival and view the landscape of our lives, the past damages due to our behavior often emerge as barriers to moving forward. We fear either rejection or punishment because of our former misuse of alcohol and other drugs.

From hurt feelings, family disappointments, to legal issues or time incarcerated, consequences carry forward in one form or another. They become either situations to manage or insurmountable barriers to a healthy and satisfying future. The choice is ours.

Initially, the work of recovery is to orient ourselves to the present and stay on a recovery path that becomes more familiar each day.

Next, we face the past from the viewpoint of the present and change for the better as a consequence. The victory, however, is not in how we mitigate past damage. The victory is in finding ourselves, restoring our inner values and beliefs, and practicing new behavior in the present.

If nothing changes on the inside, sooner or later our behavior will continue to disappoint and new damages will pile up.

On the other hand, when we change our orientation and embrace new life, positive changes emerge all around us – even as we tackle some of the tough work of life on life's terms.

The first step on the road to inside change is to answer the question, "Who Am I?" Most of us find we have buried our real selves under a ton of manipulation to get what we want when we want it – mostly in the pursuit of "more."

There is no fast track to finding oneself. It is not just a thinking exercise.

What works is developing sharing relationships with others that allows us to share our fears, dump our resentments, talk about what we most value, feel the love around us, and seek a path that lets us forgive ourselves as well as forgiving others.

Many of us emerge from this task <u>learning the benefit of a "conscious contact"</u> with a power outside ourselves, reflecting a "higher power," or eternal wisdom as we individually come to an understanding that works on our behalf. New appreciation of ethical behavior, our personal values, and ties to our individual heritage are examples of growing along spiritual lines.

The result is change – <u>change in our view of others</u> and recognition of the connectedness possible in lives of service as well as achievement. Another lasting result is finding the faith to overcome life's challenges being rewarded with growth and happiness.

A dear friend in recovery, who has passed to the beyond, often said:

"Life is all about situations. Situations can always be managed. They only become problems when I find a drink in my hand."

Tool: **ORIENTATION**
Bullet Points:

- *View your journey from a new perspective.*
- *Write down situations that could use improvement.*
- *Change your view of others.*
- *Relish new understandings and relationships.*

46.

TRUE NORTH GRATITUDE

*Gratitude makes sense of our past,
brings peace for today,
and creates a vision for tomorrow.*
o *Melody Beattie*

We begin life feeling powerful and deserving. We grow by appreciating our true strength and the value of others as well as ourselves.

Our mothers give us an early lesson in gratefulness: "Say please and thank you," we are instructed. We are taught that showing gratitude is beneficial to us. We learned with our <u>minds</u> that saying "thanks" pays off by helping us get the things we desire.

Much later, we learn with our <u>hearts</u> the larger benefit of living "gratefully." In our heart view, we are gratified by receiving attention from others. And others are gratified when we give attention to them without strings attached.

Growth is the putting aside of the concept of earned placement on this Earth, or the overvaluing of our achievement. This is True North Gratitude, the great "centering" of our core attitude toward life. We realize in our core being that gratitude is a gift, not something to be earned. We practice an "attitude of gratitude." It is proof we are innately valuable.

> *When you do things from your soul,*
> *you feel a river moving in you, a joy.*
> o *Rumi*

This growth to True North can be, and often is, interrupted by trauma, illness, displacement, war, or addiction. We bounce between fear and gratitude, forgetting for the moment that they are opposites.

When our life veers off course, we may gravitate to the ledger of cost/benefit thinking. Life becomes about what we "deserve." But remembering the roots of our journey, we sit with our supporters in recovery meetings, we visit our journals of discovery, we meditate, pray or act in other ways we have discovered that help us find our true self and our best values.

Returning, as often as necessary, to True North, we remember:

We work to pay our bills, not to enlarge our self-image.

We engage with others for mutual benefit, not to use others for fulfillment of our desires.

We treat ourselves with respect while being honest and timely in our personal inventory of assets and motives.

We accept the gift of life on life's terms, without comparison to, or judgement of others.

When we live a gratitude-centered life, our relationships are beneficial to all.

> *When you practice gratefulness,*
> *there is a sense of respect toward others.*
> o *Dalia Lama*

Tool: **GRATITUDE**
Bullet Points:

- *We learn with our <u>hearts</u> the larger benefit of living in a grateful space.*
- *We engage with others for mutual benefit.*
- *We can accept the gift of life on life's terms.*

47.

SHAKING THE FAMILY TREE

When I was 13, I sang in our church. In fact, two of my sisters and I formed the Allem Trio and sang in country churches over two counties in the Tennessee River Valley. Singing was healing in many ways I did not understand at the time, ameliorating other more challenging family memories.

But all the memories are part of me. Sealed in the work, sweat and tears of growing up. I have learned that early influences make lasting impressions because of the stages of growth and development of the brain. No other phase of life packs so much information, identifications, values and processes as the first sixty months of life.

Foremost in these early impressions are the "attachment" issues: not just the facts of our family and upbringing, but the touch, feel, sounds and experiences of our first exposure to others in the human race. Attachments range from nurturing and love, to stress and abandonment with eons of variation in between. The stories never end. And neither do the consequences of fundamental attachment.

Add to this the genetic component of life and we begin to understand the core role of family when crisis, change or growth bend the course of our lives. When life shakes us up, the branches of our life are shaken. In addition, the strain reaches our roots, and – like any tree – the health of those roots is vital to the health of the tree.

People often enter recovery in crisis. The family relationships that support each person are usually frail, torn or hidden for the individual suffering from late stage addiction illness. As recovery strategies take hold, it is useful to address the family relationships and begin rebuilding trust, responsibility, companionship and heritage.

In other words, addiction is almost always a family illness and recovery is most effective when family healing takes place. What does that look like?

First, everyone benefits from learning truth about addiction. Truth replaces society's traditional prejudice. Truth overcomes the belief that bad choices, lack of responsibility, or moral weaknesses are the cause of addiction disease. Truth includes the view that addiction illness affects everyone in the family network – some with substance using issues of their own and all with twisted thinking and feelings related to disappointment, broken trust, and actual harm stemming from chronic substance misuse.

The result is that everyone starts looking in the mirror instead of just pointing the figure of blame to the crisis-generating family member.

Second, everyone benefits from the knowledge that healing is not just possible, but probable if appropriate actions are undertaken.

Some healing occurs through actions initiated by the person in recovery. It is likely that communication will grow and that amends will occur at some point. More importantly, family members will find their own path to healing – often with a fresh understanding of spiritual tools and commitments.

As with the individual in recovery, family members will learn that connections are vital – joining in communities of family recovery. Many treatment organizations offer evidence-based practices in family healing. In addition, organizations such as Al-Anon and Nar-Anon bring family members together to share in the healing and service so vital to full recovery. Much is to be learned from books, lectures and workshops. But, as every person in long-term recovery learns, there is no substitute for learning from people who have successfully walked the path of recovery.

Every story is different. But every story helps build the next story.

Tool: **FAMILY**
Bullet Points:

- *Recognize the issues of family origins, attachments and history.*
- *Identify and serve family members in recovery.*
- *Let every healing story grow.*

48.

DIGGING FOR GOLD

"How's that working for you?"

There is a reason why that question is a favorite with therapists.

First, it demonstrates that self-improvement is a work process requiring measured results.

Second, it puts the focus on the person most likely to effect change.... Me.

Third, it illustrates the relationship between a client and therapist that achieves the best results. This relationship works the best when the therapist functions as a coach, teaching and encouraging from the bench. And the client functions as the player on the field – understanding and acting on offense and defense with appropriate, winning strategies.

My personal experience with therapy began almost simultaneous with my fifth sober anniversary. Through most of my adulthood, I had found ways to hide a core anger that had lethal potential.

"You suffer from homicidal anger," I was told. "It's a miracle you are not in jail."

That was quite a revelation for someone who had operated in the commercial world reasonably successfully for more than 25 years, assisted by significant maintenance drinking.

But he also said:

"I really like getting you guys from AA. You have the knowledge that for things to get better, you need to change. I have clients laying on my couch once a week for seven plus years who just can't get it that they have to actually change their behavior as well as their thinking."

Let's look closer at the therapist-client relationship.

MEASURABLE RESULTS – There is something business-like about engaging a therapist – even as one fears revealing the dark side of one's inner life. We are invited to share with the "coach" just exactly what a good outcome would look like. Most clinicians then share the job of laying out the work and a rough time frame. If this sounds like taking care of business, it is.

FOCUS ON WORK – My therapist would say: "Change happens in an instant. All the rest is preparation." A good building starts with a good foundation. A good life starts with healing and appreciating our core being. There is a direct relationship between how much time and effort goes into the foundation, and how long and beneficial the end product becomes. Prepare to invest real time in therapy, and don't sit down on the job.

RESULTS ORIENTATION – The partnership with a therapist is successful when it operates organically. That is, when seeds are planted and new behaviors are harvested. In between, the work of watering the garden, removing the weeds, and living in sunshine insures success.

Success in therapy is not about achieving your expectations. It is about lowering your expectations and appreciating results you never believed were possible.

Keep your therapeutic engagements to specific tasks. Complete an assignment, then think about a new engagement for a new task. When you try to control the outcomes, you are wasting time and money in therapy. When a therapist turns to judging and preaching, he or she has reached the end of this particular road. It's time to move on.

The miracle is worth fighting for. Life is invariably good. And you are intrinsically valuable.

Tool: **Therapy**
Bullet Points:

- *There is something business-like about engaging a therapist.*
- *Appreciate results you never believed were possible.*
- *The miracle is worth fighting for.*
- *You are intrinsically valuable.*

49.

A WONDERFUL LIFE

*"Just because life is not perfect does not mean
that it can't be wonderful."*

This saying, posted over the cash register of a local deli,
reminds me that my struggle for a "perfect" life is often at
odds with the facts of my life – especially my investment
(or lack of investment) in preparation, opportunity,
inspiration, and perspiration.

Letting go of the perfect and accepting life on life's terms
does not usually happen by accident. There are steps
and practices, proven over centuries, that help us learn
and enjoy our natural strengths as well as regulate our
feelings and emotions as they are challenged by the
realities of life.

Discoverying and using these tools are particularly
rewarding for individuals on an addiction recovery
journey. Foremost among these tools is a regular and
disciplined meditation practice.

"Mindfulness" is a popular practice. It amplifies our
natural, but often neglected skill for being aware in the

present – knowing what we are doing and accepting of how we are responding to what is happening around us.

This awareness, in the present, builds our capacity to see and feel the moment. We also become better aware of appropriate responses to what is happening in our inner world as well as our outer experience.

Focusing on our breath often helps in this process – linking us in the moment with our fundamental physical being.

Another practice, that I have followed for many years, is called "centering prayer." This is an "emptying" process, quieting our mind, centering in our heart, and very deliberately inviting the presence of our personal "higher power" to communion.

There are other medication practices and methods that bring the benefits of calming the moment, being open to our surroundings, and being resilient in our values and goals. Like most tools, however, they only work when we work them!

There are three useful elements in developing and maintaining a medication practice:

COACHING – Training at some level lets us hear and understand the experiences others have enjoyed in a particular practice. Coaching can occur in workshops and retreats, through web-based services, or through literature and books. Through coaching, we practice being teachable – a never-ending and always rewarding posture along the recovery journey.

GROUPS – Attending group meditation practices helps us realize the importance of setting aside specific times and making meditation something we plan for and make part of our life schedule. There is also an association of "spirit" in groups settings. We often say the sum total of spirit in the room is larger than the sum total of bodies in the room. This is both comforting and challenging.

INDIVIDUAL – The ultimate value of meditation is demonstrated in our daily, individual practice. Most methods encourage twice daily sessions when we set aside our chores, settle in a quiet space, detach from our multi-tasking brain traffic, and let our natural "awareness" skills grow and prosper.

A mentor useful in my practice always says that our brain is the most undisciplined muscle in our body. It is often in conflict with our spirit. Asking it to be quiet is not easy at first, but is less difficult with practice. Personally, I found some benefits to regular meditation relatively soon – within a few days or weeks. But the real payoffs usually begin after a few months of practice.

There is often a side benefit to regular meditation practice. Feelings from previous life scars sometimes bubble up while we enjoy a period of awareness. They can be frightening at times. Instead of responding in fear, it is useful to realize that these scars in our unconscious emerge because you feel strong and safe enough to cope with and heal from an earlier disappointment or trauma.

When challenged by a "scar bubble" during meditation, simply let the feeling pass. Don't mentally or emotionally engage or empower that feeling. Let the feeling process its way to emotional health.

Tool: **Meditation**
Bullet Points:

- *Letting go of the "perfect".*
- *Focusing on our breath links us with our fundamental physical being.*
- *The real payoffs begin after a few months.*

50.

CITIZEN JOHNNY

You must be the change you wish to see in the world.
– Mahatma Ghandi

Recovery is a system of claiming, owning, enhancing, and celebrating. It is transformative – changing our lives from self-centered, often negative and lonely experiences, to a connected and participatory exchange with our partners in humanity.

Step by step we claim, own, enhance and celebrate our place, our heritage and our role in the story.

This tool book is a useful guide to establishing this new journey. Within a couple of years, we mature as persons in long-term recovery from addiction, with our bodies restored and our minds equipped to overcome the limbic demand for stimulation. We are retooled to build lives of purpose and satisfaction.

Our spirit life is rekindled, fueling the desire, work and satisfactions of connection – with recovery partners, families, learning opportunities, our communities and our passions.

In these early months, we:

> **Claim our lives** – many of us from the brink of
> death, all of us from the bondage of craving.
> **Claim our values** – learning first that we are
> valuable and that our contributions to life and
> community are vital as they are demonstrated in
> our beliefs and actions.
> **Claim our connections** – first our early recovery
> supports, then our teachers along our path, and
> finally our associates in our work and our passions.

Too many of us stop at this level of recovery growth. We
seem secure. We enjoy life. We give back through service
in our recovery associations. We mend fences and grow
our family attentions and friendships.

What we often fail to do is **claim our citizenship**.

My life before recovery was deeply involved in political
action and policy advocacy. I left that life for a few years,
feeling that many of these associations were triggers for
my using. But I began to view the field of health, recovery,
and the vast sea of ignored pain and suffering with the
eyes of a reporter and writer. What I observed could not
be reconciled with the thinking that I should hide my
experience.

I could not get comfortable in the shame I was supposed to
quietly bear. I joined the call of former U.S. Senator Harold
Hughes, himself a person in long term recovery and
author of the historic Hughes Act officially recognizing
alcoholism as a disease. He defined citizenship as that
last right and duty people recovered from illness and

enjoying the fruits of addiction health must claim, own and celebrate.

It was clear to me that an essential part of claiming my citizenship was **claiming my voice.**

In literature for Hughes' movement, Society of Americans for Recovery (SOAR), I wrote in 1993 about "ACCEPTING RESPONSIBILITY ALONG THE ROAD OF PERSONAL GROWTH."

"Even though wide knowledge of (addiction) recovery exists, stigma and discrimination dictate much of the public policy and private attitudes.

"America, though long regarded as the most humane of nations, remains untouched by the proven linkage between treatment and lowered general health costs. And the willingness to fight drug-related crime by incarcerating addicts at $35,000 a year staggers the imagination.

"We who experience recovery too often whine: 'Why does Congress refuse to see that stigma is expensive, recovery is cheap'? Our whining misses the point. Americans are not ignorant, and our lawmakers know the facts. Americans insist, however, on seeing results.

"American voters do not "see" wellness from addiction disease. They do not see recovery because people in recovery hide their wellness. Our continuing shame defeats the cause most important to our current life and reduces hope for the next generation."

Thankfully, the view has changed since 1993. In recent years, America's community in recovery have launched a citizen movement. To use the words of Senator Hughes: We have become a CONSTITUENCY OF CONSEQUENCE.

Greg William's documentary, *ANONYMOUS PEOPLE**, and the growth of Faces and Voices of Recovery** are mobilizing tens of thousands of recovery advocates.

Those who have benefited from the "tools" of this book to transform their lives, hopes and achievements, can claim their citizenship in a variety of ways, suiting every passion, talent and life experience.

Your voices, your views and your citizenship ownership can change the health opportunity for the next generation. This is the ultimate "connection," and the endorsement of that truth: No person is an island.

* Download from NETFLIX.
** www.facesandvoicesofrecovery.org

Tool: **CITIZENSHIP**
Bullet Points:

- *Claiming, owning, enhancing and celebrating.*
- *We often fail to claim our citizenship.*
- *Changing the health opportunity for the next generation.*

Johnny Allem

A leading recovery advocate in the modern era.

- *2016 recipient of the William L. White Lifetime Achievement Award of Faces and Voices of Recovery.*
- *Member of the 2004 Institute of Medicine's historic panel on addiction health that produced* **Crossing the Quality Chasm – Adaption to Mental Health and Addiction Disorders.**
- *Featured in* **ANONYMOUS PEOPLE,** *Greg William's 2015 film celebrating the vitality and importance of the addiction recovery movement and its power to change minds.*
- *Founder and President of* **Aquila Recovery Clinic,** *a cutting edge, outpatient addiction health facility in Washington, DC.*
- *A Founder and original Board Member of* **Faces and Voices of Recovery.**
- *Author in 2004 of* **"Seven Policies to Cure Addiction In Our Lifetime."**
- *Trustee for 12 years of* **Stepping Stones Foundation,** *maintaining the home and messages of Bill and Lois Wilson in Bedford Hills, NY.*
- *Former President of* **Johnson Institute,** *featuring the pioneering work of Vernon Johnson, credited with "raising the bottom" for people entering recovery.*
- *Former Deputy Commissioner for Mental Health in the District of Columbia.*
- *President and organizer for Society of* **Americans for Recovery, SOAR,** *in early 1990s, Senator Harold*

> *Hughes' effort to mobilize the nation's recovery community into a cogent political constituency.*
> - *Practicing recovery from alcohol and other drug addiction since March, 1982.*

APPENDIX

ONE

Testimony of
Johnny W. Allem
President
JOHNSON INSITUTE
Before
The Institute of Medicine
April 26, 2004 Washington, DC

TWO

Testimony of
Johnny W. Allem, President
DC RECOVERY COMMUNITY ALLIANCE
Before the DNC Platform Hearing on Health
July 22, 2008, Alexandria, Virginia

ONE

SEVEN POLICIES REQUIRED TO CONQUER ADDICTION IN OUR LIFETIME

Testimony By
Johnny W. Allem
President
JOHNSON INSITUTE
Before
The Institute of Medicine
April 26, 2004 Washington, DC

*In 1999, the Institute of Medicine published "To Err Is Human,"
launching a major initiative to improve the quality of health
care in America. The more detailed 2001 report, "Crossing
the Quality Chasm," charted specific recommendations for
improvements in the nation's health care system. The IOM
received considerable pressure to include behavior health
systems in their review. Hearings began on April 26, 2004, by
a special IOM Committee on "Crossing the Quality Chasm –
Adaptation to Mental Health and Addictive Disorders." Five
lead-off witnesses representing the consumer communities
within behavior health were heard. Mr. Allem was the only
witness specific to addictive disorders.*

Recovery from alcoholism and other drug addiction is happening for millions of Americans – rich and poor, old and young, Ph.D.s and high school drop-outs, women and men, black and white, country and city dwellers. Achieving a stable, productive and fulfilling life is, in fact, a normal expectation when proven solutions are applied. Appropriately diagnosed and treated cases of addiction illness yield many happy out- comes:

Recovery happens. Families heal. Money is saved. Life gets better. Recovering people give back. Everyone wins!

The frequent and consistent experiences of recovery demonstrate our growing understanding of this disease and the tremendous advances of science. I believe we can say that the chronic illness of alcohol and drug addiction has been conquered. That is to say, we have proven solutions, and that when they are broadly applied, the illness can be reduced to a manageable health threat, and does not need to remain the on-going epidemic.

The fact is that when it comes to addiction, the solutions are not applied in proportion to disease prevalence. In the case of addiction to alcohol and drugs, the illness has been conquered, but the epidemic rolls on. The gap between what society knows about drug and alcohol problems and what society does with that knowledge is huge and fatal for millions.

The ground-breaking Institute of Medicine report, "Crossing the Quality Chasm," noted the importance of measurements that engage "everyone with a stake in health care." Identifying and mobilizing all available stakeholders is important to improved physical health. It is critical to improved outcomes in behavioral health and especially addictive disorders. I am grateful for this opportunity to add my voice to this effort. Thank you on behalf of myself and the millions of Americans today who enjoy recovery from this chronic, progressive and unnecessarily fatal illness.

The Johnson Institute (JI) believes recovery can become a normal and expected outcome for addictive disorders in America if and when responses are designed and applied when symptoms are presented. This appropriate application of responses in a timely manner has been a successful strategy in conquering other chronic disease. For this to occur in the early development of alcoholism and other drug addiction, significant new stakeholders must be mobilized, equipped and motivated.

Appropriate responses continue to be discovered in science and practice. New and on-going research will bring us newer and better responses. But today's challenge is to apply the responses currently available. That challenge requires new policies and practices more than it requires new science. Seven policies are required to bring the response to chemical dependency in line with other chronic ill- ness. These policies have become cross cutting principles in all of JI's projects, publications and services.

1. **Individuals and families who have survived their addiction experience must become visible and vocal stakeholders.**

History teaches us that public responses to major illness are driven by the voices of survivors, their family members and allies. We are no exception. Our society's penchant for punishment instead of treatment has choked this voice. Our willingness to see value in "deterrent" strategies instead of healing practices costs everyone.

People long in recovery from addiction find themselves banned from access to Federal education grants, loans or work assistance for a year, two years or a lifetime if they have ever received a drug conviction. More than 124,000 students have been refused financial aid or stopped applying for aid as a result of a law enacted in 1998. Banning access to financial aid unfairly punishes people a second time and denies access to education for people who are trying to improve their lives and recover from addiction. Drug convictions are the only criminal act that can take away your right to student financial aid.

More than 80 percent of those in need of addiction recovery treatment are employed. If they have health insurance that includes coverage for addiction, they frequently face limits on the amount of care and must pay higher co-pays and deductibles. More than one in five people with employer-provided health insurance are afraid that seeking treatment will cause them problems at work, including being fired, losing a license, or missing promotions. This fear of discrimination causes many to pay for treatment out of their pocket in order to avoid a claim record that includes ddiction.

The good news is that today we enjoy a generation of people in recovery that is ready and willing to speak out. The Johnson Institute was an early sponsor and funder of the Faces and Voices of Recovery Campaign, a national movement of people, families and allies in the recovery community. We must honor and support those who fight for better responses to our illness for our children and grandchildren.

In August of 2001, Peter D. Hart Research Associates conducted the first of its kind random-telephone national survey of people in recovery from drug and alcohol addiction, and family members of people in recovery. The survey showed that one in three (31%) people within the recovery community say that they definitely would be willing to speak out or write publicly about their experiences with addiction and recovery. Another third (34%) would probably be willing. Even more optimistic, half (51%) of the community felt very comfortable talking about the problems that they or their family member had with drugs and alcohol.

Eighty-seven percent of people in the recovery community say it is very important for the American public to know the basic facts about addiction and recovery. Eighty-eight percent believe it is very important for the American public to see that thou- sands get well each year. The recovery community strongly supports messages that explain results and the recovery process.

2. Address symptoms of addictive disorders when they occur.

Early awareness and early intervention lead to early recovery. That's a bargain for individuals, families, employers and society. Johnson Institute is a leader in efforts to respond to alcohol and other drug problems early on and in a range of venues.

Our health system traditionally addresses addiction when a crisis occurs: car wrecks, criminal arrests, family violence, or firing from a job. We act as though entry into detox is the beginning of the disease. And institutionally, we lose interest with- in a few months of an initial treatment regimen. I call this tendency to react to addiction as an acute ill- ness the "14-month wonder" of our health care system. Both the emerging symptoms of illness and the remarkable fact of recovery remain below the awareness level of society. Both aspects of this inattention breed the ignorance and misinformation that costs us all so much pain and money.

The seemingly radical idea that we should respond to symptoms of addiction when they present them- selves is consistent with the fact that alcoholism and drug addiction is a chronic, progressive illness.

"Brief intervention" practices demonstrate tremendous efficacy, yet are seldom applied and rarely financed by insurance or public health finance. Over a period of 6-12 months, drinkers who receive a brief intervention are twice as likely to reduce their drinking as others. United Behavioral Healthcare, a managed care organization, found that 64 percent of the people who took advantage of counseling in an Employee Assistance Program did not need further treatment to address their problem drinking. For people with high levels of alcohol dependency or addiction, brief intervention is not a substitute for treatment. It can, however, motivate risky drinkers to seek help and significantly reduce the health and other risks related to drinking.

Opportunities for clergy, school counselors, criminal justice officers and other social agents are tremendous. Simply raising the question and making conversation possible dramatically improves outcomes later in life. For instance, pastoral counselors participating in Johnson Institute's Faith Partners congregational team ministries are experiencing good results when asking this question during marriage counseling: "What role does alcohol and drug use have in your relationship?"

3. Promote healing strategies within the family and community.

Chemical dependency impacts everyone. Illness and the process of getting well have cascading impacts, moving from individuals to families, to communities, to society. Healing can, and must, include the entire family. We must carry this view into the world of healthcare reimbursement codes, workplace interventions, church ministries and schools.

Addiction is a family disease. Not only is there a significant genetic component that is passed from generation to generation, but the addiction of a single family mem- ber affects all other family members. The family environment and genetics can perpetuate a vicious and destructive cycle. Families also play a critical role in addiction recovery. They can be instrumental in encouraging a family mem- ber to seek treatment. Strong family support also increases the chances of successful recovery.

Children of addicted parents are at high risk for development problems with alcohol and other drugs. They often do poorly at school, live with constant tension and stress, have high levels of anxiety and depression and experience coping problems.

Medical costs for the entire family decline dramatically after the first year of treatment for addiction. There are fewer missed days of work and school for the entire family once an individual is in recovery.

4. Use existing institutions to intervene and promote healing.

Schools, faith-based institutions, primary care physicians, employers, the criminal justice system, and the health care system can and should recognize their stake and opportunity to identify difficulties related to substance use and developing addiction and apply appropriate educational, referral and support responses. According to research by the Peter Hart Associates for the Rush Recovery Institute (1998), American families in trouble still seek assistance and counsel from their general practice family doctor and their pastor or spiritual leader. Both of these professions report they are poorly prepared and lack knowledge or skills to appropriately respond to issues of drug use or addiction.

According to Columbia University's Center for Addiction and Substance Abuse (CASA), ninety-four percent of clergy consider chemical dependency to be an important problem in their congregations. Yet, only twelve percent of clergy have received any training on chemical dependency issues. Usually, it is family members who bring their questions and cry for help. Too often, their questions go unanswered. The pastor simply doesn't know what to do. An understanding clergy supported by committed and trained members of a congregation have a tremendous opportunity to address addiction problems in very early stages of pain.

After a decade of decline in treatment availability in America, capacity in residential and outpatient settings is growing. This is a time of opportunity. As specialized addiction treatment expands, we need to recognize the significant role that traditional institutions can and must play in ending this epidemic. Enlisting and motivating these professions requires little new money, just new attitudes, training and commitment.

5. **Restore responsibility for addiction recovery within the nation's private health care finance system.**

Prevention, treatment and recovery are health responsibilities. Eighty percent of people in need of treatment are employed, most with insurance benefits. Yet, most employee-based insurance hinders people from being treated successfully for addiction. Lifetime limits are imposed on episodes of care even though addiction is a chronic disease, much like asthma, diabetes, and hypertension. Treatment is arbitrarily reduced or terminated for people with addiction disease, despite recommendations and standards of care providers. And by not fairly covering addiction treatment, like other chronic illnesses, insurance companies discourage people from seeking treatment by making them pay more out-of-pocket expenses.

Today, taxpayers are the single largest funder of addiction treatment services. Individuals pay almost eight percent of the cost of treatment out-of-pocket. Private health insurance only make up about 35% of the funding for addiction treatment. It's called dis- crimination! We must access the traditional health care dollar. That's why JI supports Members of Congress like Rep. Jim Ramstad (R-MN) and Rep. Patrick Kennedy (D-RI) and the work they are doing with the H.E.A.R.T. Act. The cost transfer of chemical dependence to the public sector delays appropriate care, costs much more, and reduces the chance for recovery. Access to the traditional, private health care dollar must be granted, if the addiction epidemic is to be over- come. The epidemic cannot be stopped with government money and self-pay treatment alone.

Studies have shown that the costs of chemical dependence treatment parity are minimal compared to the cost of untreated alcoholism and drug addiction. Treatment for alcoholism and drug addiction saves the healthcare system through lower primary health care and reduced accidents alone, not including the positive effects on lives, families, and communities.

A Minnesota report found that almost 80 percent of the costs of addiction treatment were offset in the first year following treatment due to decreased use of hospital, emergency room, and detoxification services and reduced arrests. In California, a study found that criminal activity declined by 66 percent, drug and alcohol use declined by 40 percent and hospitalizations declined by 33 percent following treatment.

Requiring health insurers to honor appropriate health claims is too often discussed as a cost issue rather than a discrimination issue. Cost is simply not the issue. Projected costs on data from states than have enacted parity for treatment have found the average premium increase due to full parity would be 0.2%-0.5%. The costs of addiction in America far exceed the minimal costs of enacting the HEART Act.

6. **Rebuild and reward a qualified, professional workforce for specialized treatment of addictive disorders.**

The professionals who staff specialized addiction treatment are highly motivated but under rewarded. Consequently, the turnover of staff is among the highest in the health industry. This workforce operates detoxification centers, intake and assessment clinics, residential treatment, intensive outpatient treatment, and specialized clinics and service centers. They include methadone clinics, collaborative services for people with co-occurring disorders and senior services. The field has experienced intensive pressure to upgrade education and technical credentials in recent years. The effort, however, is not met with increasing pay or opportunities for promotion. Individuals who obtain advanced degrees or credentials are drawn to other health fields for better income and professional growth.

According to estimates of the Association for Addiction Professionals, the majority of addiction recovery workforce is aged 40 to 55 years old. Most report spending less than half of their time counseling, often spending 60% of their time doing paperwork. Counselor turnover is more than 50% each year. In a March, 2004 survey, The Lewin Group reported that 5,000 new addiction professionals are needed each year just to replace those who are leaving the field.

The majority of people entering the field are drawn by personal factors such as their own personal experience with addiction, a family member's experience with addiction, or the desire to help the community. Challenge, desire, community, family issues, and training are all listed as reasons for entering the field by professionals, well ahead of the opportunity for advancement and pay. We are grateful for the missionary aspect of people entering the field, but the career outlook is devastating and must improve.

Positions in the chemical dependency field must be appropriately paid and honored. Low salaries are cited by 84 percent of hiring managers as the reason they cannot fill these positions.

7. The spiritual gateway to change and healing works.

The acknowledgement of the importance of faith practices is a door opening perspective, not a narrowing of the view. Trouble people and families turn to their institutions of faith for help. Too often, pastors and congregations lack the knowledge to help.

There is no conflict between science and spirituality, only misunderstanding and intolerance. Research continues to demonstrate the positive relationship between spiritual practices and values and evidence-based scientific practice. Pastors and spiritual leaders who study addiction disease and appropriate health responses dramatically increase possibilities of recovery.

The power of prayer to promote healing is well documented. In a Duke University study in 2001, a cardiac care group subject to off- site intercessory prayer had 50% better outcomes and fewer complications than those patients that were not subject to intercessory prayer. At the same time, a variety of paths and combinations of therapies and medication are effective and need support as appropriate responses for many individuals.

Civilization is blessed with a variety of physical specimens, personalities and states of mind. The universality of addiction disease is apparent. Just as apparent is the need, and the supply of varied and flexible recovery responses.

From the cross-cutting principles I have outlined, let me address the three specific questions you have posed.

> 1. *In what ways does substance use disorder health care diverge from these aims for quality health care (safe, effective, patient-centered, timely, efficient and equitable)?*

As I have documented, the current system of health response to substance use disorder begins in crisis, applies acute care regimens, fails to provide long term support and blames the patient for relapse rates that are in fact lower than the rates for asthma, hypertension and diabetes. Though most professional, intensive treatment for the crisis phase of illness is adequate for this advanced state of illness, the health care response overall is not safe, effective, patient-centered, timely, efficient or equitable.

> 2. *What strategies should be employed to improve these defects in health care quality?*

The strategies we support are:

- Moving recognition and response to the earliest presentation of symptoms;
- Engaging ancillary professionals (such as clergy, school counselors, police, human resource, etc.) in knowledgeable responses – including intervention and referral;

- Honoring and engaging people who have survived their experience with addiction illness; and
- Restoring appropriate reimbursement for addiction treatment from traditional healthcare plans, where premiums have been paid with the expectation of appropriate care.

   3. *What roles should consumers play in improving the quality of substance use treatment services?*

Consumers undergoing treatment for crisis symptoms are not likely to become a viable force for better treatment as long as early difficulties are ignored, crisis difficulties are punished and survivors discriminated against. We need to end discrimination, apply healing technologies where appropriate and honor and respect recovery.

May I add that this institution and this forum can significantly enhance America's view of this dis- ease and advance the range of responses. As a person in recovery, I am grateful for your attention to behavioral health generally and addiction recovery specifically. I am honored to be part of this process. A prevailing view is that stigma is the primary barrier to appropriate attention and care. That may be true. But I suggest that fighting stigma is like packaging fog. What we can really work on is practices that end discrimination and policies that expand vocal and effective stakeholders. Your process has the hope of improving both.

Thank you for this opportunity to testify on behalf of Americans who suffer this disease and those who have recovered successfully.

TWO

"IT COULD HAVE GONE THE OTHER WAY."

<del>◄ımı∬ıııı►</del>

Testimony of
Johnny W. Allem, President
DC RECOVERY COMMUNITY ALLIANCE
Before the DNC Platform Hearing on Health
July 22, 2008, Alexandria, Virginia

My name is Johnny Allem and I enjoy long-term recovery from the disease of alcoholism. That specifically means I have not had a drink or drug in 26 years. I am very happy with this outcome. So are my family, neighbors, and the tax payers of the District of Columbia.

I have been an active advocate for fresh and science-based policies for addressing addiction in America since 1985 when I was appointed chair of the Mayors Advisory Council on Alcoholism in the District of Columbia. I speak out to demonstrate recovery and advocate so others may enjoy the benefits of recovery as I have.

While I have a story of spectacle and bad behavior as is often played up in the media view of this disease, my larger story - like millions of Americans - is one of service, responsibility, joy, and citizenship. I have been a successful businessman in the District, a cabinet member in DC Government, operations director of the District's mental health system, and president and CEO of a national non-profit organization.

I have written, testified, and demonstrated on behalf of addiction recovery and the larger field of behavior health and public health. In a national program known as Recovery Ambassadors, I have taught more than 2500 citizens in recovery how to be citizen advocates.

Fourteenth and V Streets, Northwest, in Washington, DC, is today in the heart of a gentrifying and thriving inner city neighborhood. On the northwest corner, however, is the worn and drab building more indicative of the neighborhood's history since the 1968 riots. Next to a deli on the corner is an unmarked door. The door opens to a narrow and dingy stairway with well-worn treads, stained walls, and the light of one 60-watt bulb.

A sign at the top of the stairs welcomes you to a twelve-step clubhouse. From 7 am to nearly midnight, hundreds of District residents climb these steps, walk down the hall to a coffee room, and spend a few moments in fellowship and gratitude for another 24 hours without a drink or a drug. The air is really different inside the club. It is weighted with the kind of gratitude only the dying can appreciate. To express this gratitude, someone several years ago pasted a homemade poster along side the official welcome sign at the top of the stairs. It simply said:

"It could have gone the other way."

In 1991, I was the alcoholic in recovery that first walked those stairs, signed a lease, and helped others organize a recovery club on that corner. I cannot describe the gratitude I feel as I meet those who began their recovery journey at 14th and V over the past 17 years.

But let me share an even more potent story for me:

Last Saturday, my son held a huge party at his home in Fairfax County. It celebrated his daughter's 14th birthday. This wonderful child, my oldest grandchild, has never seen her grandfather drunk. I am reminded that my grandfather died of this disease much younger than I am today. Her grandfather is alive, healthy, productive to society, and made her favorite home-made ice cream for her birthday party.

I testify today not just on behalf of the millions of Americans who enjoy recovery as I do. I testify today on behalf of my three grandchildren, and the offspring of alcoholics and addicts everywhere. The science is clear. I know where their genes come from. I work so help will be there for their generation.

The science has taught us so much. But no disease in modern America has such a gap between what science teaches us and how we respond to illness. When I began my journey in 1982, I was told that many die without any intervention and most wind up in institutions and jails.

It is not any better today. In fact, in the same decade that has seen the most advances in brain science is also the decade in which America built more jail cells per capita than any civilization in history – largely to accommodate crude and inappropriate drug penalty laws.

The work of the 1990s has left us a horrible legacy. But it has produced one positive result: Today, American voters favor treatment – not jail – for people suffering with an addiction diagnosis.

I am reminded every day that I have choices. I choose to tend to my recovery because I know that "it could have gone the other way."

In America, we have not chosen recovery. Our story is going the wrong way. My grandchildren and your grandchildren will pay for our wrong choices. Those of you who craft policy for government action can make different choices.

That is why I and the DC Recovery Community Alliance strongly endorse the three-point platform recommendation of the Whole Health Campaign outlined here today:

1. Ensure equitable and adequate mental health and addiction treatment coverage in all public and private health care plans.
2. Support policies that promote individual and family recovery from mental illnesses and addictions as integral to overall health.
3. Commit to investing in America's future through prevention, early intervention, and research on mental illnesses and addictions.

Together, we can choose to recognize and honor recovery and the millions of citizens who enjoy successful outcomes from addiction disease.

We can choose to mainstream responses to addiction and mental illness so early symptoms are recognized and addressed.

We can choose to end the no-end, no-win, so-called War on Drugs and stop the expensive, corrosive and even racist jailing of Americans without attention to their primarily addictive conditions and illnesses.

We can choose following science to normalize recovery – moving addiction from an epidemic to a manageable health threat.

We can choose a healthy America – saving lives, saving money, restoring integrity and meaning to the American dream.

Let's not lose this opportunity to follow science, to follow success, and to follow the good sense of American voters.

Let's go the right way, the healing way, the recovery way.

Thank you.

END

CPSIA information can be obtained
at www.ICGtesting.com
Printed in the USA
LVHW02s1736240118
563777LV00002B/2/P